The Unequal Hour

"A rich man once said, "*It's easy to make more money, but you can't make time*". Time is the ultimate non-renewable resource. These days everybody complains about time scarcity, yet Strazdins reveals how inequalities in people's access to time reflect broader injustices in society. Her analysis of time provides a unifying theme for understanding the origins of health inequalities".

—Ichiro Kawachi, John L. Loeb and Frances Lehman Loeb
Professor of Social Epidemiology, Harvard University

"Lyndall Strazdins henceforth is a Time Lady—or Lord, whatever the past masters of *Doctor Who*'s planet Gallifrey deem appropriate. She is the first in our universe to set out temporal issues as both determinants and consequences of individual and community health.

Take your time to read this wonderfully elegant short time and health volume. It will yield more time. Don't believe any other sci-fi characters (like Commander Deanna Troi in one of the better Star Trek capers, First Contact) who would say "*This is no time to talk about time. We don't have the time!*"

This concise and comprehensive essay is, indeed, bigger on the inside—it will give you more time. It will give new insights for our complex understandings of time, money, health and well-being. It is, in fact, possibly high time to be published".

—Evelyne de Leeuw, *Professor of Public Health, School of Public Health, University of Montreal, holder of the 'Canada Excellence in Research Chair' in One Urban Health, Professor of Urban Health and Policy, University of New South Wales*

"I'm very pleased to see this new book by Professor Strazdins. Inequalities associated with access to time and control over time have received too little attention from work-family researchers. This very thoughtful 'deep dive' to consider the expansive impact of such inequalities on all aspects of life has the potential to influence the work of many researchers".

—Shelley MacDermid Wadsworth, *Distinguished Professor, Department of Human Development and Family Science and Director Emerita, Center for Families; Director, Military Family Research Institute, Purdue University*

"Lyndall Strazdins' brilliant book demonstrates that time can kill, time can stress us and time can make inequality worse. In a nutshell she conceives time as one of the most pressing health issues of our time. This important book also offers prescriptions for institutions, corporations and governments about how time pressures can be reduced to improve health. Make the time to read this book for your health's sake!"

—Fran Baum, *Professor of Health Equity, NHMRC Fellow and Director of Stretton Health Equity, University of Adelaide*

"This is a timely book in every way! In a period where questions about work, efficiency, fertility and health are on policymakers' minds around the globe, Lyndall Strazdins shows the connections between time and health for all people, genders, workers and students. Strazdins not only explains the price of time and the links to health outcomes and inequality, but she also provides examples of policies and practices that can change the way we use time and improve our lives".

—Marian Baird AO, Professor of Gender and Employment Relations, Co-director of the Sydney Employment Relations Research Group, University of Sydney Business School, editor of *The Multigenerational Workforce: Managing Age and Gender at Work* (2024) and *At a Turning Point: Work, Care and Family Policies in Australia* (2024)

Lyndall Strazdins

The Unequal Hour

How Time Is Shaping Health

Lyndall Strazdins
National Centre for Epidemiology and Population Health
Australian National University
Canberra, ACT, Australia

ISBN 978-981-97-6336-8   ISBN 978-981-97-6337-5   (eBook)
https://doi.org/10.1007/978-981-97-6337-5

Cover pattern © Melisa Hasan

This Palgrave Macmillan imprint is published by the registered company Springer Nature Singapore Pte Ltd.
The registered company address is: 152 Beach Road, #21-01/04 Gateway East, Singapore 189721, Singapore

If disposing of this product, please recycle the paper.

To the people who give time to others. This book is a small token of gratitude.

Preface

We communicate, travel, process data and generate information at orders of magnitude faster than any point—ever—in human experience. Everything is speeding up, yet most people still feel the need to do more. But is there is a limit to how fast or how much people can do, and is this limit their health?

What people do with their time reflects—deeply—who they are. However, time is about more than a choice, a job or a gift of love—it is something needed for good health. As a health promotion leader told me "in health terms, time is almost like a prescription...like two fruit, five veg...and thirty minutes of physical activity" (Fig. 1). There is a problem however, as too few people are 'taking time for their health'. Almost two thirds of early deaths worldwide are from chronic diseases such as diabetes type 2, cardiovascular illness and many cancers. Most of these deaths could be prevented by exercising more and eating healthier food. But many people don't do nearly enough of these two simple things, even though they know they should. So why is this? Is it because they are lazy, unmotivated, ignorant or is time for health a resource only some have? What if chronic diseases, obesity rates, cancer and many other health conditions are all, partly, malaises of time?

Understanding and addressing this necessity—to have time for health—is what this book is about.

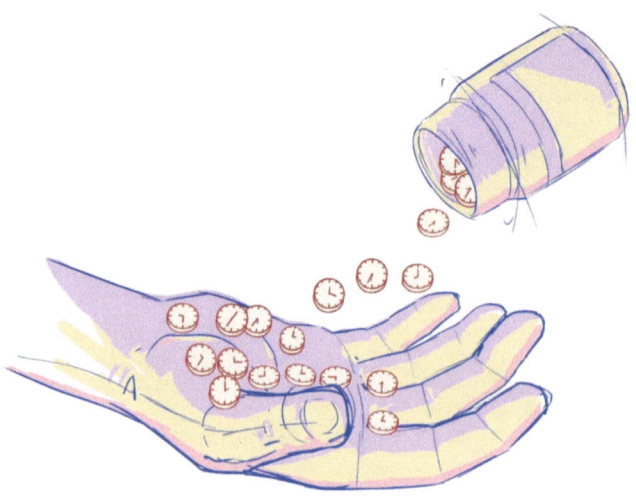

Fig. 1   A health prescription. Erin I Walsh 2024

Health care experts have not found a way of helping those who cannot find time to eat well, exercise or get enough sleep. Health and medical experts do not understand why people are saying they don't have enough time, nor are they paying attention to solving it. Policymakers care deeply about taxes and budgets, but almost never pause to consider how their decisions affect time. The default has been to assume everyone has enough time, they just need to be told (again) how they should spend it to stay healthy. From doctors to politicians, it is assumed everyone can do what they please with their time and so everyone can find enough time for health.

This book is for anyone who cares about health (their own or others), and anyone who cares about social justice. My ambition is to introduce ways to think about time and then describe why it is so important for health. This is the focus of the first two chapters. Further, not all of us can use our 24 hours, every day, in the same way. Just like money, some people have plenty of time they can use for their health, but some people have very little—these are people who are less powerful, whose time is not counted or poorly paid, and they are very often women. How time is embedded in social and health inequality is therefore the focus of Chap. 3. Chapter 4 then presents examples of actions and principles to help readers, policymakers and health experts address time shortages and protect health.

I hope this book helps you understand why we need to think differently about time if we want to address chronic diseases. Most of all, I hope you are enriched and provoked by these ideas, because time is a concept that is poetical, practical and deeply political.

P.S. I have also tried to keep it brief, knowing how time stressed you may be.

Canberra, ACT, Australia   Lyndall Strazdins

Acknowledgements

This book is a product of many fine minds—my family's, colleagues' and friends'. I'm confident I could not possibly list everybody.

I thank and acknowledge the intellectual input, creativity and make-it-happen energy of two extraordinary scholars, Eliza Martin and Amelia Yazidjoglou. They have helped me wrangle this book and without them it would not have happened. They've given me intellectual insights into my sometimes old-fashioned thinking, urged me to see points of view I had missed and generally did a huge amount of careful checking and literature review. They certainly gave a lot of time and I'm incredibly grateful for their collaborative help.

I want to thank my university—the Australian National University—and my school—the National Centre for Epidemiology and Population Health—which has been my scholarly home. They have supported me to do this work, including time off from a busy job as part of a visiting fellowship to Harvard. I would also like to thank Ichiro Kawachi and Harvard T.H. Chan School of Public Health who generously hosted me and made my (what seemed far too brief) stay such a pleasure. Meanwhile Darren Gray, Peter Ward and Sharon Alberto held the fort while I was away. Thank you.

Where I live and work is Ngambri and Ngunnawal Country, a land that has been cared for and connected with for millennia. I am grateful to this land, its First Nations caregivers and custodians, and to the deep understanding (and willingness to give time) that such care and connection requires.

The ideas in this book have been a slow burn, fuelled by collaboration with exceptional thinkers. Tessa MacDonald worked with me on the very first iteration of this idea which we called the 'time kit'. There have been two women academics who have been my guiding lights throughout my career, Dorothy Broom and Gabriele Bammer. Thank you for showing me what was possible. I've worked with exceptional scholars and collaborated with them on many of the projects which this book is built from. Jane Dixon, Cathy Banwell, Jenny Welsh, Ginny Sargent, Liana Leach, Jianghong Li, Christine La Bond, Sharon Friel, Michael Bittman, Huong Dinh and Tinh Doan. These sociologists, anthropologists, implementation scientists, epidemiologists and economists made me think differently and far better. The Australian Research Council made this research possible with their Linkage LP160100467, LP100100106, Discovery DP190100975 and Future Fellowship FT110100686 awards.

I would also like to thank the wonderful, creative team at the school—the PHXchange—especially Erin Walsh, whose beautiful illustrations are in the book. They bring creativity, imagination and vibrancy to the scholarship of many people here on campus, including mine. I am also indebted to Gordon Harrison Williams whose fine graphic-artistry inspired the vision for this book.

There have been other guides I've relied on too. Romy Katz and Janet Smith, thank you for keeping me focused on what matters. And I appreciate the patient willingness of the team at Palgrave Macmillan, especially Marion Duval.

Of course, none of this would have happened without the love, thoughtful minds and hilarious humour of my family. Thank you, Tim, for reading drafts and for your grounded, insightful, plain language edits. My daughter Carla, whose ideas, enthusiasm (and astute observations) kept me going. My son Dan once wrote me a sticky note saying, "you can do it", it was a long time ago, but the sweetness of that message has stayed with me.

Contents

About the Author

Lyndall Strazdins is a Professor at the Australian National University. A recipient of the ARC Future Fellowship and the Marie Skłodowska-Curie International Fellowship Seal of Excellence, she is widely known for her work and family scholarship. Strazdins leads research on time as a social determinant of health and combines clinical psychology with population health approaches. She is the mother of two lovely, grown-up children and is a very sedate horse rider.

List of Figures

1

Time: Thinking About Time—It's Complicated

Abstract Ideas about time have preoccupied philosophers, scientists and writers. This chapter introduces time as a social concept. Time is like money in one way—it's a thing people need and use for just about all aspects of daily life that enable good health. But, unlike money, food, water or shelter, they can't see or touch it, it is not a tangible thing. Time is elusive, and personal but this also means it is easily overlooked even while daily lives are controlled by it. Essential ideas about time are summarised and linked, drawing from political economy, sociology and economic insights. Different facets of time are explained, beyond the assumption time is just hours and minutes. As well as connecting time and money through the historical process of industrialisation, the chapter explores new experiences of time through technology and the speeding up of daily activities, including recent framings of modernity as social acceleration.

Keywords Efficiency • Intensification • Social acceleration • Time use

Ideas about time have preoccupied philosophers, scientists and writers, with one of the best academic texts about time (and sociological analysis of time) by Barbara Adam (2004). In her book, Adam describes the many different dimensions to time and how the way people think about time has changed from when seasons drove how each day was spent to, nowadays, clocks. This chapter introduces ideas about time relevant to health—drawing mainly from authors such as Adam in sociology, political economy, economic and feminist scholarship. I hope to show that just about all aspects of daily life are shaped and ordered by time, but unlike money, food, water or shelter, we can't see or touch it, it is not a tangible thing. But we can feel time, we use time and we obey time. We anticipate time, allocate time, count time, exchange time for money, seek to keep to time and almost everybody organises their days and lives in terms of hours, minutes, schedules and timetables. Hours and minutes don't tell the whole story, however.

1.1   A World Without Clocks?

Imagine a world without clocks. Most people consider time to be made up of seconds, minutes and hours. Yet this way of thinking about time, in terms of human history, is new. Time was not always measured by clocks or precisely quantified, although all cultures have had some way of marking the passage of time, whether this be days, months, seasons, planets, lifetimes or years.

Early mechanical clocks emerged in Western society during medieval times, although Islamic cultures had been using accurate water and sundial measures for centuries before (McFadden, 2019). Starting in churches and palaces, then town squares, clocks evolved to become ubiquitous features of houses, workplaces and eventually apparel. Since everyone had the same time, measured in the same way, clocks also allowed ordering, synchrony and scheduling. They defined when to start and stop tasks or activities, as well as the measuring of the working day. Clocks enabled transport, production, trade and communication to scale up and speed up, creating efficiency and an economic reach that would have been previously impossible.

The invention of steam engines is widely viewed as the catalyst for industrialisation in the modern economy. But, steam engines and the railway only became economically potent because of clocks and the mechanical measurement of time on which systems and timetables were built. This mechanisation and counting of time eventually became global and universal so that all nations followed a similar time accounting system, which is still adhered to in the twenty-first century. The setting of Greenwich Mean Time in the 1830s was the first step, enabling British railways to synchronise, powering the industrial revolution in that country. Globalised time was the next step. In the 1884s, the Prime Meridian was established at the International Meridian Conference, which set a standardised time system across the globe. Although it took decades more to be implemented by all countries, the adoption of the universal, clock-based time counting system was one of the key technological innovations that underpinned globalisation as well as industrialisation. How we think about and respond to time is, therefore, a profoundly socially, economic and historically shaped process—it is neither immutable nor fixed, a point particularly important when it comes to considering policy.

1.1.1 Time Discipline

The invention of the clock changed the meaning of time, as well as how time was measured (Adam, 2004). It moved time away from agrarian meanings of seasons, dawn, noon, dusk, day and night to a regular, mechanical, precise and socially synchronised measuring that never varied. This standardised time was crucial to industrialisation, because it meant that time could be counted and exchanged for other quantified resources, especially money.

Because time became the key ordering concept for how business ran and days were kept, a 'time discipline' needed to be imposed (Thompson, 1967). Time discipline refers to the way in which daily life is ordered by and subordinated to clock time. Thus, the time when people start and stop work, complete tasks or attend meetings can be measured to the minute, as is the timetabling of transport. Time discipline is learnt. It starts in schools or perhaps earlier. Children are not born with an inherent sense of clock time, they learn within families, in schools and in almost all daily transactions the importance of being on time and the consequences of disobedience to keeping time.

Time discipline is a daily experience, so pervasive that most adults don't notice or question it. Cultures of punctuality vary by nations, however, and correlate with the degree of marketisation and economic development (Levine & Bartlett, 1984). In South Korea, for example, there is a culture of 'pali-pali'—it means simply—quickly-quickly. Doing things faster, hurrying and not wasting time is an unmistakable feature of Korean society. This drive to be faster and do more means, as the website observes, Koreans walk fast, drive fast, eat fast, deliver fast, communicate fast. Time, and the clock, are one of the most important structuring characteristics of behaviour in contemporary societies. It is logical that time will be a powerful influence on health.

The banner below and others like it came from the time rights movement for an 8-hour working day. Australia was a vanguard in this respect. Over 170 years ago Australian stonemasons won the right to a 48-hour, 6-day working week with Saturdays off. It was a pivotal point in industrial relations, a world first, and achieved through mass working hour marches and protests. The marches continued though, and it took another 100 years before an 8-hour workday and 40-hour week became standard in Western countries. The movement, and the banner, divided the 24-hour day into three—asserting that everyone had the right to 8 hours for rest and 8 hours for recreation. This meant work hours should be limited to 8 hours a day to achieve this. But there is something they left off the banner, and that is the time needed to care (the extra eight added to the image) (Fig. 1.1).

1.2   Time and Money

Being able to count time meant it could be given a commercial value, and this became the foundation on which market economies ran. As Marx observed, the exchange of time for wages defines a fundamental social relationship—earning a livelihood rests on it. Employees doing more work in less time also drives up profit, motivating business to put pressure on increasing time while minimising money paid, to increase

Fig. 1.1 Eight-hour work-day banner. Noel Butlin Archives Centre, Australian National University: Australian Insurance Staffs' Federation, E98-87, banner, single-sided, gold crepe paper eights sewn onto blue fabric, 65 × 107 cm, unknown date, 1920–1960

efficiency and stay competitive, so that "moments are the elements of profit" (Marx, Capital Vol 1, P366).

The terms of the time–wage exchange at the foundation of the labour market creates and embeds relative power. That is, how many hours must be worked, and how hard one must work, to earn how much money, by whom. Thus, privileged and well-educated workers earn more money for their hour than the unskilled or low educated. Men earn more than women, white people earn more than people of colour and so on (Keeley, 2015). Time and money combine to create privilege as well as underscore and embed it. For the less privileged to earn more they must work longer or faster, and this is one of the mechanisms of time-based inequity that then plays out in worse health. Thus, time can be thought of as a flip side of income—it is in constant tension and a trade-off with money. People can use time to earn money, and money can be used, at least to some extent, to buy time through purchasing services, hire nannies or buy labour-saving devices.

There is a clear, two-way relationship, but time and money are not the same things. Anyone who goes to an airport, for example, will witness the neat petitioning of status that is repeated throughout the journey. People pay more for first-class, business or premium seats and for their money, they don't only receive prestige and quality they also buy themselves time. Their queues are shorter, and service is faster. Status is marked by deference or more comfort, *and* it is demonstrated by quickness and command over time. Most wait, but the privileged do not. This is a social process that plays out in myriad daily events, from queues in shops to waiting lists in hospitals, a winnowing of importance and power though the value given to people's time. Yet, analyses of class, poverty and socio-economic relationships with health have focused almost entirely on income and education, missing the crucial role that time also has in defining people's choices, power, actions, opportunities and health.

1.2.1 Economics and Time

Not surprisingly, given the importance of time and money to profits and pay rates, economists have been thinking about time for decades. Gary Becker, a Chicago economist and Nobel laureate, argued that time (saving and spending it) was as important as money in driving consumption and behaviour. It is a calculation that sits behind the concept of 'opportunity cost', where people weigh up forgone time as well as forgone money when they make choices about what to do or buy. Again, this is an insight that our health system has misunderstood, as if just by telling people to spend more time on their health, their behaviour will change in a healthier way. But, in a society where time is valued like money, we are putting a 'price' on health for people to pay. If this was costed in terms of money, it would be clear that such a price is easier for some to afford compared to others (just like income-poor people are unable to afford high-quality health care).

In affluent societies that have embraced the notion that time is money, everything that takes time is viewed as a cost; even private decisions such as what is bought, what is eaten, what is cooked and what is wasted are made through the lens of time. Becker observes,

> Americans are supposed to be much more wasteful of food and other goods than other persons in poorer countries, and much more conscious of time: they keep track of it continuously, make (and keep) appointments for

specific minutes, rush about more, cook steaks and chops rather than time-consuming stews and so forth. They are simultaneously supposed to be wasteful—of material goods—and overly economical—of immaterial time. Yet both allegations may be correct and not simply indicative of a strange American temperament because the market value of time is higher, relative to the price of goods there than elsewhere. That is, the tendency to be economical about time but lavish about goods may be no paradox, but in part simply a reaction to a difference in relative costs. (Becker, 1965, pp. 513–514)

The full cost of an activity, including any activity to maintain health, includes its market price (in terms of money) *and* the forgone value of the time it uses. And, if people earn more for their time—it becomes more valuable. Like with money, as time becomes scarcer, its relative value also increases (Aguiar et al., 2011; Alonso, 1964). Thus, behavioural economists Anuj Shah et al. (2012) have shown that under scarcity—either time or money—decision-making changes dramatically. People become preoccupied with what they lack, and overestimate time costs of activities when under time pressure, just as they overestimate financial costs when under financial pressure. This then creates a short-term decision framework. Thus, both affluence and time scarcity drive up the value of time and its importance to people's lives and choices. For example, an Australian behavioural economics team found the average Australian would pay AU$68 for one extra hour of time in a day, which is well above the average hourly pay rate. But among those most affected by time stress (young women) an extra hour was worth even more, valued at AU$131 (NAB Behavioural and Industry Economics, 2018).

In Becker's theory, households are "producing units" and "utility maximisers" (Becker, 1965). They combine time and market goods to produce more commodities, for example, cooking a meal involves purchasing food (money) plus the time involved in choosing the meal, shopping for ingredients, preparing the food, eating it and then cleaning up (Heckman, 2015). The financial cost is mainly evident at the point of shopping, but the time cost occurs through almost all aspects of household production and consumption. Households choose the best combinations of income, time and goods to maximise other things that they can produce and consume to maximise their happiness. This theory does not really grapple with the value and imperative that people place on time for care, nor does it account for time for health and rest, which is largely considered under the umbrella term "leisure" (Blundell & Macurdy, 1999).

1.2.2 The Birth of Public Health?

Even though public health has failed to recognise the importance of time for health, centuries ago, Marx did not. He wrote "the working day has a maximum limit. It cannot be prolonged beyond a certain point......This maximum limit is conditioned by.... the physical bounds of labour power. Within the 24 hours of the natural day a man can only expend a definite quantity of his vital force. A horse, in like manner, can only work from day to day in like manner, 8 hours. During part of the day this force must rest, sleep; during the other part this man has to satisfy other physical needs, to feed, wash and clothe himself" (Tucker et al., 1978, p. 362). Thus, health is intrinsic to power relations in the labour market and its value in terms of time is reckoned into the workday. Marx argued that the time–income exchange includes health in a three-way trade-off, otherwise the workday had no limit except 24 hours.

At the time of Marx's writing, there was virtually no regulation of working hours. Workers competed for jobs, while work weeks ranged upwards from 58 hours. Men, women and children sold their time to earn income to avoid destitution, since apart from poor houses there was no welfare system. The impact on health was visible, especially children's health, with deformities, injuries and disease commonly observed, and work time became the focus of social reformers (Engels, 1958). Thus, the Factory Act of 1833 was passed after a Royal Commission into Working Conditions, whose key regulations were about time. The Act forbade the employment of children under the age of 9 (except in silk mills). Children aged between 9 and 13 years were not allowed to work for more than 48 hours a week or 9 hours a day, while young persons aged from 14 to 18 years were not permitted to work for more than 69 hours a week, or 12 hours on any one day. The minimum break for meals was fixed at 1½ hours a day, and night work for all persons under the age of 18 was forbidden. At the same time, it was made compulsory for children under the age of 14 years to have 2 hours of schooling each day (Engels, 1958). Further regulation of women's and young persons' working time then followed in 1847, with the 10 hours bill limiting their (but not men's) hours of labour. Nowadays, child labour is viewed by the ILO as a violation of human rights; it remains, sadly, an endemic problem in some countries, driven by deep poverty.

The birth of public health is often ascribed to the insights of Dr John Snow, who, in 1854, realised the high importance of clean water and sanitation for controlling and preventing the spread of cholera. His identification and disabling of the Broad Street Pump as the source of a cholera outbreak marked one of the first and most famous public health actions recorded. Equally though, in terms of health, the regulation of work time should be celebrated and lauded: these laws improved the lives and circumstance of vast numbers of people; early social policies which surely had an enormous impact on population health.

1.3   Not Just Hours and Minutes

So far I focused on work hours, which Adam (2004) refers to as aspects of time *duration* (how long, often measured in hours and minutes). But, there is more to time than hours or minutes, and these other dimensions are important for health.

1.3.1 Speed and a New Virtue of Efficiency

In a study of six countries several decades ago, Robert Levine and his colleagues observed that the fastest walking speeds were in Japan, followed by England, North America, Italy, Taiwan and Indonesia (Levine & Bartlett, 1984). These differences in walking speed were striking. Japanese pedestrians walked nearly a fifth faster than the average Indonesian. Levine calculated that walking speed or hurriedness corresponded with the degree of economic and technological development. What he discovered was that 'pace of life', that is, how fast we do things, is a characterising feature of cultures, economies and points of history. Speed is social.

Marx also understood how important pace and speed was, believing it to be as important as work hours in the wage–time exchange. Thus, people could also work faster to produce more goods and improve their pay. How long people work and how fast they work can be interchangeable. One reason why work hours have gone down over the past century is that productivity per working hour has gone up. Part of this productivity is due to technological advances and mechanisation, and part is due to increased work speed. Efficiency has become a virtue we ascribe to. But it was not always the case.

Adam Smith, in 1776, realised that specialisation saved time (Smith, 1776). But, it was Frederick Winslow Taylor (1911) who perfected efficiency, changing the speed of work—and therefore our lives—when he developed a way of organising production called scientific management. Taylor inspired a whole new way of thinking about work, which was to calculate the quickest way to produce a good or service by breaking down the steps into quick, repeat actions. For example, instead of one worker overseeing the production of metal parts from being poured to being cooled, shaped and then finished, production was broken down into steps. Each step was then performed by one worker, or a small team, to produce that part at the fastest possible speed, transforming how long each product took to make. Taylor saw this as an unprecedented improvement for everyone. Employers dramatically reduced their costs. Workers were given better wages because of improved output. And, the much lower costs of production meant that consumers could buy products that they would never previously have been able to afford. In fact, the social good of efficiency was a key argument put forward by Taylor "the greatest prosperity can exist only when [an] individual has reached his highest state of efficiency: that is when he is turning out his largest daily output" (Taylor, 1911).

Taylor's efficiency delivered affluence to huge numbers of the population by making goods cheaper and wages better, and this underpinned improvements in health. The whole basis of mass production and automation (taken to the next stage by Henry Ford) was based on Taylor's insights and methods of efficiency. But, these financial gains came at the cost of an altered experience of time.

Efficiency as an economic principle puts time and amount produced as the superordinate determinants of performance and a prosperous, virtuous life. Even for nations. National productivity, for example, is calculated as gross domestic product per hour worked, embedding time in its measurement. But it did not come without a cost. Taylor (1911) describes how he reduced the workday of ball bearing inspectors from 10½ to 8½ hours with a regular break. They were not allowed to talk or interact and could earn much higher wages if they worked fast. He selected young women with the capacity to very quickly inspect the ball bearings, which drastically reduced the workforce needed, and increased output, while improving wages and reducing hours. But, it changed the way that they worked—social time and enjoyment were removed because it slowed down output. Working as fast as possible was expected, while control over time was reduced. The principal of efficiency fully commodified time in the workplace, it became an input and an evaluation. The purpose of work was to maximise production, irrespective of minds, bodies, enjoyment or equality (all of which matter to health). Scientific management enabled mass production to develop. It improved the standard of living for the working and middle class in ways that had not been imaginable before. At the same time, keeping a job became a tournament of working faster or longer, as employers sought the quickest workers, not just the most skilled (O'Neill & O'Reilly, 2010). Now, the constant drive for efficiency is still having a negative impact on both mental and physical health (Airila et al., 2014; Boxall & Macky, 2014; Macky & Boxall, 2008; Moen et al., 2013; Murcia et al., 2013; Stansfeld et al., 1995; Volkoff et al., 2010; Zoer et al., 2011). There is little sign that work pace (also called intensification) is slackening (Green, 2004).

The power of efficiency as an organising social principle has moved far beyond the workplace. It characterises governments (the Australian government periodically has what is called efficiency gains, where it cuts budgets but not workloads), cities (one of the key performance indicators of the Smart City movement is to save 100 hours of citizen time in a year), how fast we walk (Levine & Bartlett, 1984) and even families (Brown & Warner-Smith, 2005). Dale Southerton (2013) documents the way family life has become harried. By harried, he means people—especially women—struggling to compress more tasks within limited time frames while simultaneously feeling burdened and anxious about meeting needs. Tasks are combined, such as cooking a meal while helping children with their homework. Harriedness or rushing becomes embodied; it connects a different quality and experience of time with a corresponding change in behaviour, embedding economic and social demands to do more into behaviour, biology, physiology and mental health (Krieger, 2014). Doing one thing at a time has become a luxury for many, multitasking has become normal. Asking people, then, to allocate more time to health (it takes nearly an hour and a half to complete 10000 steps a day, walking moderately fast, and this is what is recommended to keep healthy) is asking many to do what is almost impossible. Health is competing for time in a scarce market.

1.3.2   Time Control and Social Status

"Q: If you have to make a choice between work and another (family) activity, how do you make that decision? A: How do I make it? Normally it's work that's the overriding factor, there'll just be -- I think it's just a weighing up of what will be the impact on work if I don't, if I have to leave early from work to do something which is not work-related, it's a matter of weighing up how big is the impact going to be, can I live with the impact?" (unpublished interview with a manager, Jane Dixon and Lara Corr, "Contestations over work time: Should health weigh in?").

Being able to control one's time is a form of sovereignty. It reflects choice about when to do things and for how long, being able to vary start and stop times, deciding when to have breaks, take holidays, or even how long the workday is. Having control over time may be just as important as how much time people have, at least in terms of supporting good health. As I discussed earlier, people are held to account for their time, and wasting time (and other people's time) has become a contemporary sin. This time discipline is especially visible (and enforced) in the workplace, but control over time is also socially patterned. It varies with type of job, privilege and the types of demands people are facing. One of the markers of high status in workplaces is the ability to control workflow, including being able to delegate work to others. Some jobs, especially those which involve a high level of interaction such as in health, aged or childcare services, or serving people in shops or at counters also have low time control because people's needs and demands are often urgent. When someone is ill, distressed, in need or waiting for service, responses must be as fast as possible and can't be deferred. Outside the workplace, caregivers and parents lack control because their routines, schedules, time allocations and choices must all be made in reference to the needs of those they are caring for.

This interplay between time control and social status is most visible in the workplace, and it is important because it shapes the opportunity to carve out predictable, plan-able time for healthy living and accessing health care. Joan Williams et al.' (2013) theory of flexibility stigma argues that in most countries there exists the expectation that work should have priority over people's time. She calls this "work devotion schema", it includes time discipline, and it is expected. Anything that disrupts availability for the job is seen to be challenging devotion to the job. This creates penalties to enforce control. Flexibility, as well as not working long hours, are seen as a lack of devotion. This is one reason why family-friendly provisions—such as being able to vary start and stop times, leave work early, work from home or work part time—have not been widely taken up, especially by men. Even though being available to attend special events, respond to unexpected care needs or simply spend time with children matters deeply to parents and caregivers, most people continue to fit family needs around work, rather than vice versa. And, they have rational reasons for doing so, because challenging works' moral right over our time attracts penalties, either in terms of keeping a job, or advancing careers (Coltrane et al., 2013; Williams et al., 2013).

Although this moral duty to devote our time to paid work prevails for everyone, privileged workers still have more (and different) types of control. Both class and gender are stitched into this mix. High status jobs (such as managers or professionals) usually have flexible hours, although it is accompanied by the expectation of a stronger devotion to work. This expectation is particularly strong for men and weaker for women. Men's work devotion in these high-status jobs is seen to justify their better pay and signal their elite status, a badge of class and superiority. In these jobs, work hours do not define the workday, because work does not end until the task does. These men work long hours, are paid well and occasional flexibility is accepted. But mostly, when flexibility is used by men, it refers to extending work into family time such as working back to finish a task, not vice versa (Dixon et al., 2019).

The time requirements of low-wage and low-status jobs, at least in the developed world, are quite different in how they challenge control over time. Typically, these jobs do not require long hours, they are often short or unpredictable. Thus, job insecurity in terms of income is paralleled by insecurity and unpredictability of time. The just-in-time approach to organising business has a powerful flow-on to control over time, because people may not know when they need to be available for work. For these jobs, the penalty is not about how long people are expected to be working, rather the penalties centre on availability when required. Even if only offered part-time work, these low-wage workers are expected to be available all the time. If they are not (because of care or juggling another job to make ends meet) they typically get less work, and therefore less income. Among the less privileged, time is on standby, availability is expected, but payment is unpredictable. This not only disrupts availability to be caregivers, with flow-on to children's health and development, but also the routines and planning needed for exercise, or preparing fresh food.

There are also many low-wage workers who must work very long hours to earn sufficient money, often in multiple jobs. These working-poor lack both money and time and define a group of individuals and families who are among the most exploited and vulnerable. For these people, taking time for health care, looking after children, the elderly or sick, or taking time for exercise and healthy eating is even more difficult. Their disadvantage generates ill health as well as the opportunity to prevent or treat it. It is therefore a mistake to assume those who are income-poor are time-rich. Even if part-time, many people's time is on call. The same goes for people who are caring for others, often on welfare—their time is also on call. Yet, most health care services for the income-poor, as do most programmes of preventative health, assume time (including wait time) is not a problem for low-income people.

1.3.3 Unsociable Time: It Matters When We Do Things

"I do 12-hour shifts, so it's 6:00am-6:00pm or 6:00pm-6:00am, every two shifts…. I'll get home in the morning, at 6:00am. If my kids are up, I'll give them breakfast and so forth, and then I'll go to sleep. Then I'll wake up at 4:30 pm, shower, get ready, and then leave to start work at 6.

So I'll only ever see them maybe for a half hour in the morning or a half hour when I wake up. And that's if they're home" (36-year-old blue-collar father, unpublished interview, Jane Dixon and Lara Corr, "Contestations over work time: Should health weigh in?").

In the post-war period, a standard work week was defined as 8 hours per day, 5 days per week (Costa, 2000). Sunday work was restricted and work performed on weekends, evenings or nights attracted extra pay. Some shift work occurred, especially among manufacturing, mining and construction industries (blue collar) attracting overtime pay to supplement relatively low wages. This was before the growth in service jobs, and before digital technology meant that business could be transacted every hour, any hour, anywhere. This has profoundly shaped the timing of work, meaning work outside standard hours is common among many workers. Shop hours are a good example. On the one hand, being open on weekends and late into the night (sometimes even right through the night) gives opportunities and choice for when people can shop. But on the other hand, it has changed work time dramatically. Legal restrictions on night and weekend opening hours have been systematically lifted in the US, Canada the European Union and Australia (Richter, 1994). In many of these countries, the extra pay that was previously granted for working outside Monday to Friday was also deregulated. Now, what is called an ordinary span of hours can be anywhere from six in the morning to midnight, and work shifts can start or stop any time in the span without attracting extra pay. People are paid the same money if they start at 6 o'clock in the morning or 9 o'clock, or if they end their shift at midnight or at 5 o'clock.

In fact, the idea that work time has boundaries at all is being tested. Now that digitisation allows remote working, people can work or be asked to work wherever they are, and at any time. For the more privileged white-collar workers, this offers flexibility of time and increases choices, but changes the timing of work and workplace expectations. People can choose when or where they do their work, but this generates a creeping expectation for work 'out of hours'. This downside is called technology intrusion, whereby people feel they cannot or should not be away from their job and are constantly checking emails or calls. In some countries, notably France, Belgium, Portugal and most recently Australia, right to disconnect laws have been passed to try and protect time away from work, although the onus is mostly on the worker to refuse to take calls or respond to emails out of hours, rather than on employers to desist. But not everyone can use technology to increase their choices—for many, especially blue- or pink-collar workers, jobs require them to be in a specific place, at a specific time, rarely of their choosing. Thus, blue-collar men's leisure time is more fragmented, as they often work in a trade or in manual jobs which are inflexible and shift based; they have less time on weekends, and it is often broken into short periods. Although white-collar (high paid) men work long hours during the weekday, they have longer periods of uninterrupted time on weekends for rest, leisure and to be with their family (Chatzitheochari & Arber, 2012). This means they can also plan or leverage time towards healthy behaviours such as exercise or food preparation, in ways blue-collar men cannot.

Timing and scheduling also affect synchrony, which is the capacity to match your time with other people's—another way time affects health. Social relationships, companionship and nurturing are among the most important of all resources for health. Relationships take time, and the time they depend on must be synchronised. People need enough time to build and maintain strong relationships at work and outside of it, and parents need time to raise children. Therefore, it is not just the amount of time, but the ability to control and synchronise it that is important, as the father who works shifts (quoted above) reveals.

Timing is everything, because time has a social and shared meaning as well as a market meaning. If you have free time, but it's in the middle of the night, then the ability to use that time, for example, to go for a walk, or hang out with your children is quite different to having free time in the day. Broken short time periods are hard to redirect or plan, and unpredictable time disrupts habits and routines that are essential for most healthy behaviour. Yet, public health has not only ignored how important time is to reduce disease burdens and live well, it assumes that, if there is any time free it could and should be used for health. Thus, when we interviewed public health leaders, if they did recognise time barriers to health behaviours, they also believed that people could find time, all they had to do was switch time from, for example, watching TV. This is the most common objection made to the idea that there are time constraints on people's health—hours spent viewing TV are invariably cited. Switching time is true if the time people use to watch TV is equally able to be used for exercise. It's not true if the only time you have free is in the evenings, or after dark, if you live in a neighbourhood where you feel unsafe, or if you must be available and in the home because of children.

1.3.4 Conflicted Time

"I really want to have a time where we sit down at the table as a family, at dinner. Because that's what I did growing up and so that will force me to committing to at least a number of days a week (at home) to be doing that" (White collar, employed father, unpublished interview, Jane Dixon and Lara Corr, "Contestations over work time: Should health weigh in?").

One in eight Australians say they lack work-life balance (ABS, 2018). In the EU, it is closer to one in five (Masevičiūte et al., 2018). What people mean by 'work-life imbalance' is that they either lack time, or the time they devote to one valued activity prevents them from devoting time to another or they are so tired from one role that they cannot do the other. As expected, this is bad news for health. Difficult choices are made among competing priorities, and dilemmas and conflicts grow. Even as people do one thing they feel guilty and worry that they should be doing another (Southerton, 2013), time conflicts become a source of anxiety. This is particularly obvious when two powerfully valued and time-consuming activities clash; it's what most people mean when they talk about work-life balance. Because, along with its market value, time has other values and uses, a point Marx and the political economists missed. Time is also a marker of love, care and commitment; this kind of time is hard to buy, it's personal, and it's precious. In fact, if people did not give time to care for and connect with others, the social and economic fabric would collapse. Raising children takes time, as does giving or receiving support, and it's hard to imagine social capital—that collective, relational web of networks that is a powerful driver of health and well-being (as well as economies)—ever occurring without people investing time. Nancy Folbre, a feminist economist saw what Marx missed, and she describes these time investments as the invisible (economic) heart (Folbre, 2001). The work of care, love and tending to others is the foundation for any social order and functioning economy, now or future. Time equates with love, not just money, creating dilemmas about how to manage both. Almost anyone who combines work with care, be it for a child or a family member who is ill, disabled or frail, and in Australia this is four out of ten of all workers (ABS, 2018), is likely to experience multiple, daily time conflicts. Sometimes these time conflicts are sudden, huge and a shock. Becoming a parent, a sudden illness in the family, an accident, moving house—what psychologists call 'life events' almost always require a major shift in time, sometimes, but not always short lived.

Time at work competes with the obligation and deep human longing to spend time with family, especially children, and it's a social problem that has become a major focus of science (Greenhaus & Beutell, 1985). Sociology, psychology and family scholars describe how work-family conflicts affect people's health and well-being, including children's (Strazdins et al., 2012). Mostly, the problem is conflicting time, although another element is when worries, moods or preoccupations cross from one domain to another. Most often, conflict over time is seen as a problem for women, which it certainly is, but it is also a problem for men. Kerry Daly, a Canadian fatherhood scholar (1999) shows that these days, fathers face conflicting imperatives to earn money and be breadwinners even while they are expected to put children first (Daly, 1996). So important has time become to family life that almost all decisions centre on time. When Daly interviewed fathers, he found that they view their performance as workers *and* as parents through the lens of time. Were they giving enough time to work or their children or were they stealing time when they shouldn't? Time has become a currency through which most people make decisions about love as well as work; this generation of fathers, like mothers, are living with a temporal conscience (Daly, 1996).

1.4 Social Acceleration

Two hundred years ago, steamboats would take 4–6 weeks to travel from Pittsburgh to New Orleans and 4 months to return. Now, the journey by air is a matter of hours and minutes, while communication between the two cities is instant (Cowan, 1997). Hartmut Rosa (2013) argues that the defining feature of modernity is not industrialisation or digitisation, efficiency or even globalisation, it is acceleration. It has come through technological innovation (to which clocks were instrumental) and the pressures of market capitalism to use time as a resource to be maximised, and these combine to create something that is far bigger. As I wrote in the preface, we now communicate, move and travel, process data and generate information at orders of magnitude faster than at any point—ever—in the human experience. This reduces the time it takes to do almost everything, but rather than freeing up time, it simply makes things happen faster. This applies to everything, from the individual action to the global transaction. People even eat fast (Anekwe & Zeballos, 2019). It also raises the expectation (and need) to do more (Wajcman, 2015).

Speed and acceleration is deeply transformational. As one of the leading sociologists writes "the acceleration of molecules can transform ice into water into steam…. changes in the temporal structures of modern society [can] transform the very essence of our culture, social structure and personal identity" (Rosa, 2013, p. 17).

Social acceleration is ongoing, it hasn't peaked. If speed and quickness, saving time and efficiency, continue to be desired, it is likely to continue. Speed sells, and each innovation breeds the need for more speed, affecting almost all aspects of lives and livelihoods (Scheuerman, 2020). Acceleration is evident in the (increasing) pace and tempo of how things happen, and it also shows up in instability and fracturing of time. Episodes of things can be far shorter—news comes in soundbites, often just an image. Emails interrupt. Multitasking speeds up the experience of time as well as tasks and is a response to the need to do more. We no longer have typing pools, instead we have computers. Digitisation and word processing have made writing and communicating faster—we don't need typists—we do it ourselves. So, as things occur faster, people respond by doing more, and more quickly, while the expectation for what could or should 'be fitted in' grows. Acceleration and time pressure are not necessarily gauged by whether there are hours and minutes 'free' from work or care or other commitments. Instead, expectations and practices expand so that the free time becomes something felt to be wasted, inefficient or better directed to the multitudes of other opportunities, or distractions. Time is not a thing we have but a thing we use, and as social processes around us speed up, it creates a different feeling about time. Rushing, even if it is episodic, becomes common. Paradoxically, this creates fatigue. Will people use their 'free' time to exercise or source, prepare and clean up after a healthy meal? Will they use it to rest and recover from a rushed day? Or will they use it to do more, because they feel they should?

1.4.1 Change Is Getting Faster Too

However, it's not just how fast people do things that are different, acceleration has changed the way societies work and this has major implications for governments and policymakers, who are important allies if we wish to address time for health. Social change is faster, generating perceptions of instability and uncertainty, even while everyday actions have become far more complex, adding further 'drag'. Rosa argues that we are making decisions that are increasingly reactive and short term. Planning is harder. Time frames and turnarounds are shorter. Even political decisions have accelerated. A truly democratic process involves consultation and deliberation, as does sound policymaking (Scheuerman, 2020). This is time consuming, and increasingly less feasible as the pressure and the need to respond to social change and events speed up. Anticipating the future and preparing for it is harder to do; meanwhile, changes in social orders are occurring at ever shortening spaces of time. People (and policymakers) want quick fixes; they seek and rely on technical solutions to growing disease burdens, narrowing policy options and ability to address root causes. There is this interplay. Speeding up of lives is partly driven by technology, partly driven by our appetite, or is it a fetish, with efficiency and doing more in less time? (Wajcman, 2015).

Social acceleration sums up the effects of equating time with money, the constant 'mining' and maximising of time as an economic resource, and the impact of technological advances that have emerged out of industrialisation. There has been a change in the entire social fabric, a temporal spiral of wanting and valorising efficiency and speed, even while it pushes human limits—physical, mental and social.

1.5 More to Time

There is more to time than what I have described, so I end this chapter with a short commentary on other elements of time that matter to health, some of which I pick up in the next chapter. I start with Nancy Krieger's eco-social theory (2014) which articulates how health is shaped within a web of influence. Her theory is largely considering racism but can be applied to sexism and indeed all forms of privilege and un-privilege. She argues that oppressive social relations are embedded in how institutions operate and how resources are distributed. This flows through multiple levels that combine to alter individual circumstances, resources, opportunities and freedoms and all of these become embodied in individuals' minds, emotions and biology. This embodiment is what constitutes health.

This systematic directing of opportunities and harms is evident on multiple scales, daily, over the life course, affecting individual lives and bodies even as it is directed at a social group. This can be deliberate or unconscious. It can be explicit or simply embedded in the rules, culture, day-to-day acceptances of how things work. As I've hoped to show, time is intrinsic to structures in the labour market, in the household, in the way economies, cities and workplaces function. But, there are other aspects of time I have not foregrounded, yet are important (Gee et al., 2019).

1.5.1 Time from Past to Future

One aspect of time that I have not given emphasis to, is time as it unfolds over the life course. What has happened in the past is shaping, and to some extent determining, our health in the present and what may happen to our health in the future. There is a chronology to health, especially chronic health conditions, which may take many years to manifest. Being unable to exercise on one day is unlikely to change health alone. Being unable to exercise for a year, or even a decade is when the health harms start to show.

This is a particularly important aspect of time for health because social opportunities and achievements, as well as health, evolve. There are trajectories whereby what happened in the past sets the course for what can happen in the future. A child who lacks a safe, nourishing and responsive environment will set in train a cascade of physiological and psychological processes which will develop—over time—to alter life chances as well as health status as they grow up and then begin to age. This is called cumulative disadvantage and has a clear time dimension. Connected to this idea is the idea that the longer people live, the more opportunity they have to be 'exposed' to harms that will have a health impact. Privilege can protect people from health-harming experiences, while discrimination 'weathers' people. There is wear and tear on bodies and minds that is connected to oppression and exclusion. Gee et al. (2019) note, for example, that African-Americans have shorter cell telomeres (a sign of accelerated biological ageing) (Geronimus et al., 2010) as well is shorter life expectancies (Gee et al., 2012). So, there is a time dimension to other health hazards, even while time (or its lack) itself shapes health directly.

1.5.2 Lost Time

Gilbert Gee et al. (2019) in their perceptive analysis of time and racism, articulate another way time connects to health. Until now, most of my examples have focused on the way time resources, be it control over time, demands on time or valuing of time is systematically patterned by gender and socio-economic status. I have, however, also described the way time signifies power and privilege. Gee shows that it is also systematically patterned by race and that time can be used as a tool of discrimination. He uses the term "lost time" as another marker of disadvantage. For example, he cites evidence that cars take longer to yield to African-Americans wanting to cross the street than they do to white Americans (Roy et al., 2004). African-Americans need to wait longer in queues to access health care than their white counterparts (Liederbach et al., 2015; Pettigrew, 2017). African-Americans spend a far longer time in prison for the equivalent crime, relative to whites (Yang, 2015). Every example he gives has a linkage to health because their effect, from day-to-day slights, delays, barriers, dismissals, to being punished longer, accumulate and create time-based opportunity costs that are socially and systematically loaded. Racism, and sexism, and most forms of privileging can happen through time, by taking away time, by costing time, by using time as a penalty or by undervaluing and dismissing some people's time relative to others.

There are new demands on time, and public health professionals, as well as policymakers, have misunderstood them. We have viewed time as something an individual has and can spend as they wish—time is all in the mind. We imagine that once informed of the need to do so, people will redirect time to their health. The field has not realised how much time has changed, or how hard it is for many people to control. Although we have accepted that time is one of the most important inputs to the economy and our jobs, we have failed to recognise it as an input for health. Nor has public health realised how important time is to poverty, inequality and privilege, and that it combines other socially patterned resources to entrench them. We have framed disadvantage largely in terms of money, or education, and missed seeing the added significance of time. As George Eliot observed "Time, like money, is measured by our needs" (P135, Middlemarch 2015 edition, first published 1871–72).

References

ABS. (2018). *4125.0 – Gender indicators.* Australian Bureau of Statistics.
Adam, B. (2004). *Time.* Polity.
Aguiar, M., Hurst, E., & Karabarbounis, L. (2011). Recent developments in the economics of time use. *Annual Review of Economics, 4*(1), 373–397. https://doi.org/10.1146/annurev-economics-111809-125129
Airila, A., Hakanen, J. J., Luukkonen, R., Lusa, S., Punakallio, A., & Leino-Arjas, P. (2014). Developmental trajectories of multisite musculoskeletal pain

and depressive symptoms: The effects of job demands and resources and individual factors. *Psychology & Health, 29*(12), 1421–1441.

Alonso, W. (1964). *Location and land use. Toward a general theory of land rent.* Harvard University Press.

Anekwe, T. D., & Zeballos, E. (2019). *Food-related time use: Changes and demographic differences. Economic information bulletin 301136.* United States Department of Agriculture, Economic Research Service.

Becker, G. S. (1965). A theory of the allocation of time. *The Economic Journal,* 493–517.

Blundell, R., & Macurdy, T. (1999). Labor supply: A review of alternative approaches. In O. Ashenfelter & D. Card (Eds.), *Handbook of labor economics* (Vol. 3, Part A, pp. 1559–1695). Elsevier.

Boxall, P., & Macky, K. (2014). High-involvement work processes, work intensification and employee well-being. *Work, Employment and Society, 28*(6), 963–984.

Brown, P., & Warner-Smith, P. (2005). The Taylorisation of family time: An effective strategy in the struggle to 'manage' work and life? *Annals of Leisure Research, 8*(2-3), 75–90.

Chatzitheochari, S., & Arber, S. (2012). Class, gender and time poverty: A time-use analysis of British workers' free time resources. *The British Journal of Sociology, 63*(3), 451–471.

Coltrane, S., Miller, E. C., DeHaan, T., & Stewart, L. (2013). Fathers and the flexibility stigma. *Journal of Social Issues, 69*(2), 279–302.

Costa, D. L. (2000). The wage and the length of the workday: From the 1890s to 1991. *Journal of Labor Economics, 18*(1), 156–181.

Cowan, R. S. (1997). A social history of American technology. *OUP Catalogue.*

Daly, K. J. (1996). Spending time with the kids: Meanings of family time for fathers. *Family Relations,* 466–476.

Dixon, J., Banwell, C., Strazdins, L., Corr, L., & Burgess, J. (2019). Flexible employment policies, temporal control and health promoting practices: A qualitative study in two Australian worksites. *PLoS One, 14,* e0224542. https://doi.org/10.1371/journal.pone.0224542

Engels, F. (1958). *The condition of the working class in England.* Basil Blackwell.

Folbre, N. (2001). *The invisible heart: Economics and family values.* New Press.

Gee, G. C., Hing, A., Mohammed, S., Tabor, D. C., & Williams, D. R. (2019). Racism and the life course: Taking time seriously. *American Journal of Public Health, 109*(S1), S43–S47.

Gee, G. C., Walsemann, K. M., & Brondolo, E. (2012). A life course perspective on how racism may be related to health inequities. *American Journal of Public Health, 102*(5), 967–974.

Geronimus, A. T., Hicken, M. T., Pearson, J. A., Seashols, S. J., Brown, K. L., & Cruz, T. D. (2010). Do US black women experience stress-related accelerated biological aging? *Human Nature, 21*(1), 19–38.

Green, F. (2004). Why has work effort become more intense? *Industrial Relations: A Journal of Economy and Society, 43*(4), 709–741.

Greenhaus, J. H., & Beutell, N. J. (1985). Sources of conflict between work and family roles. *Academy of Management Review, 10*(1), 76–88.

Heckman, J. J. (2015). Introduction to a theory of the allocation of time by Gary Becker. *Economic Journal, 125*(583), 403–409. https://doi.org/10.1111/ecoj.12228

Keeley, B. (2015). *How does income inequality affect our lives?* OECD Publishing.

Krieger, N. (2014). Got Theory? On the 21st c. CE rise of explicit use of epidemiologic theories of disease distribution: A review and ecosocial analysis. *Current Epidemiology Reports, 1*(1), 45–56.

Levine, R. V., & Bartlett, K. (1984). Pace of life, punctuality, and coronary heart disease in six countries. *Journal of Cross-Cultural Psychology, 15*(2), 233–255.

Liederbach, E., Sisco, M., Wang, C., Pesce, C., Sharpe, S., Winchester, D. J., & Yao, K. (2015). Wait times for breast surgical operations, 2003–2011: A report from the National Cancer Data Base. *Annals of Surgical Oncology, 22*(3), 899–907.

Macky, K., & Boxall, P. (2008). High-involvement work processes, work intensification and employee well-being: A study of New Zealand worker experiences. *Asia Pacific Journal of Human Resources, 46*(1), 38–55.

Masevičiūtė, K., Šaukeckienė, V., & Ozolinčiūtė, E. (2018). *Combining studies and paid jobs: Thematic review.* EUROSTUDENT.

McFadden, C. (2019). *The very long and fascinating history of clocks.* https://interestingengineering.com/the-very-long-and-fascinating-history-of-clocks

Moen, P., Kelly, E. L., & Lam, J. (2013). Healthy work revisited: Do changes in time strain predict well-being? *Journal of Occupational Health Psychology, 18*(2), 157–172.

Murcia, M., Chastang, J.-F., & Niedhammer, I. (2013). Psychosocial work factors, major depressive and generalised anxiety disorders: Results from the French national SIP study. *Journal of Affective Disorders, 146*(3), 319–327.

National Australia Bank Behavioural & Industry Economics. (2018). *NAB well-being insight report. Time: How we use it & value it.* National Australia Bank.

O'Neill, O. A., & O'Reilly, C. (2010). Careers as tournaments: The impact of sex and gendered organizational culture preferences in MBA's income attainment. *Journal of Organizational Behaviour, 31*, 856–876.

Pettigrew, S. (2017). The racial gap in wait times: Why minority precincts are underserved by local election officials. *Political Science Quarterly, 132*(3), 527–547.

Richter, P. (1994). Seven days' trading make one weak? The Sunday trading issue as an index of secularization. *British Journal of Sociology*, 333–348.

Rosa, H. (2013). *Social acceleration: A new theory of modernity.* Columbia University Press.

Roy, K. M., Tubbs, C. Y., & Burton, L. M. (2004). Don't have no time: Daily rhythms and the organization of time for low-income families. *Family Relations, 53*(2), 168–178.

Scheuerman, W. E. (2020). *Liberal democracy and the social acceleration of time.* JHU Press.

Shah, A. K., Mullainathan, S., & Shafir, E. (2012). Some consequences of having too little. *Science, 338*(6107), 682–685. https://doi.org/10.1126/science.1222426

Smith, A. (1776). *An inquiry into the nature and causes of the wealth of nations: Volume one.* W. Strahan; and T. Cadell.

Southerton, D. (2013). Habits, routines and temporalities of consumption: From individual behaviours to the reproduction of everyday practices. *Time & Society, 22*(3), 335–355.

Stansfeld, S. A., North, F., White, I., & Marmot, M. G. (1995). Work characteristics and psychiatric disorder in civil servants in London. *Journal of Epidemiology & Community Health, 49*(1), 48–53.

Strazdins, L., Lucas, N., Shipley, M., Mathews, B., Berry, H. L., Rodgers, B., & Davies, A. (2012). Parent and child wellbeing and the influence of work and family arrangements: A three cohort study. *FaHCSIA Social Policy Research Paper*, (44).

Taylor, F. W. (1911). *The principles of scientific management.* Harper & Bros.

Thompson, E. P. (1967). Time, work-discipline, and industrial capitalism. *Past & Present, 38*(1), 56–97. https://doi.org/10.1093/past/38.1.56

Tucker, R. C., Marx, K., & Engels, F. (1978). *The Marx-Engels reader.* Norton.

Volkoff, S., Buisset, C., & Mardon, C. (2010). Does intense time pressure at work make older employees more vulnerable? A statistical analysis based on a French survey "SVP50". *Applied Ergonomics, 41*(6), 754–762.

Wajcman, J. (2015). *Pressed for time: The acceleration of life in digital capitalism.* University of Chicago Press.

Williams, J. C., Blair-Loy, M., & Berdahl, J. L. (2013). Cultural schemas, social class, and the flexibility stigma. *Journal of Social Issues, 69*(2), 209–234.

Yang, C. S. (2015). Free at last? Judicial discretion and racial disparities in Federal sentencing. *The Journal of Legal Studies, 44*(1), 75–111.

Zoer, I., Ruitenburg, M., Botje, D., Frings-Dresen, M., & Sluiter, J. (2011). The associations between psychosocial workload and mental health complaints in different age groups. *Ergonomics, 54*(10), 943–952.

2

Health: Time as a Resource for Health

Abstract The most common reason people say they don't exercise or eat healthy food is lack of time. The author reframes time as a resource needed for health—like money—but not every hour is equal. There are misconceptions that there is plenty of time for health; the problem is poor choices or laziness, driving a commonly held view that instead of watching TV everyone should just get off their couches. The author presents notions of usability of time, asking if free time is available in a decent chunk, can it be used safely and by whom? As well as summarising evidence on time and health links, the author explores six potential pathways: a health hazard; as a barrier for healthy behaviours; as a trade-off with family care or work; as an element of social weathering; a mechanism of social exclusion and finally as a keystone connecting social power to health inequality.

Keywords Health behaviour • Health hazards • Health inequity • Social weathering • Work hours

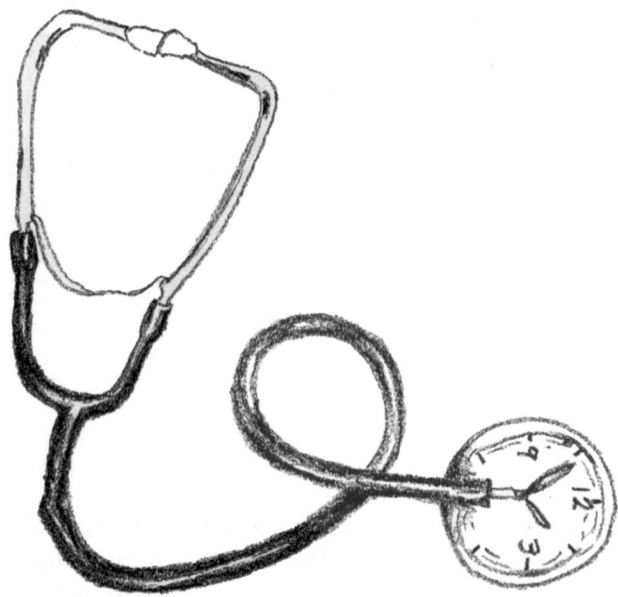

Fig. 2.1 Stethoscope. 2024 Author

As Chap. 1 revealed, time is a complex concept and can be thought of in many ways. I don't discount this complexity at all. However, when thinking about the link between time and health (Fig. 2.1), I believe it is easiest if we consider time as a resource people need. It helps to think about time like we think about income, at least up to a point. Just as income is understood as a valuable and finite resource for health, so too is time. And, it gives a good analogy because everyone accepts that people vary in how much income they earn, and understands how closely money and power are connected. There are decades of research showing how important income is for health, which further builds the case. Also, a commodified understanding of time prevails—time is money—so framing time as a resource meshes well with this and makes it easier to argue for its value. Scambler (2007) uses the term "asset flows" in a similar vein, arguing that assets and how they flow between people are the media of class relations and power (he didn't list time). Like money, time has a superordinate relationship and can drive decisions across multiple aspects of people's lives. Like a lack of money, lack of time drives choices (go for a walk or stay back at work; buy fresh or fast food) that matter for health. However, I need to make an important distinction about time as a resource for health. Usually, the problem of lack of time is viewed as a problem of lacking 'free' hours and minutes, which is time free from other duties and demands. This is one of the perils of framing time as a resource—as a sort of temporal currency—to fit with economic thinking. This is because the principle of efficiency treats all hours and minutes as the same, 15 minutes at midnight is equal to 15 minutes at midday, and if people have the time to surf the Internet or watch TV, then surely they should use that time for their health. This assumes that each minute or hour is exchangeable and equivalent in what it can produce or be used for—this is one of the ways time differs from money. So, free time is often viewed as leftover time, or spare time available for health—but it isn't, at least not always. Let me explain.

2.1   Useable Time

Although every hour is made up of 60 minutes, not all hours and minutes are equally useful. Time's usability depends on the control people have over what they can do with that time. For example, is it available in short fragments of a few minutes, or can it be interrupted and easily disrupted? Similarly, does that 'spare' hour occur when and where people can take advantage of it (e.g. midnight vs midday), or does that hour need to be kept available for other demands (even if these demands are hard to predict or uncertain)? This is a critical point on not only how we think about time and health, but how we might intervene to promote better health. Health experts, governments and in fact many people make assumptions that time for health is any time left over from 24 hours minus time that is contracted (paid work, commutes) or committed (household work, caring for others) (Strazdins et al., 2016). Sometimes personal care (sleep, bathing, eating, dressing etc.) is added into the equation.

It is often argued that if people have even 15 minutes of free time, then they should and could be using it for their health—they have no excuse.

Thus, it is claimed that watching TV is wasted and unhealthy time and a testament to people's laziness or poor choices (it does increase risk for cardiovascular disease, obesity and mortality) (Dunstan et al., 2010; Hu et al., 2003). I agree that sedentary time has increased, because jobs are sedentary, travel is sedentary and leisure often is too. I also agree with the evidence that sedentary time can be unhealthy. In fact, I urgently believe people need to spend more time being active. But, when you dig into the time-use patterns of people who watch television, the peak viewing time is after work, between 8 and 10 p.m. (US data). Hardly anyone watches TV in the morning, and it starts to creep up as the day progresses. Evenings are the times (if people are parents) when children are home and can't be left unattended. This is a time when it's usually dark, so going for a walk or a run is very different than if it was in daylight, especially in some neighbourhoods and for women (Sugiyama et al., 2007). People are more likely to be tired in the evenings, some are also eating dinner, washing up and doing their ironing while they watch TV. About half of TV viewing is spent with other people, so there is often social interaction, which is also valued and a priority (Krantz-Kent, 2018).

2.1.1 Factors Which Influence Usability of Time

The notion of usability picks up on the other dimensions of time discussed in Chap. 1. When people have 'spare' time, their ability to use it for health depends on much more than how long that time is. It will depend on their ability to synchronise with activities, people or schedules, on having control, whether the time is uninterrupted or predictable or if it needs to be kept available, such as a shop worker waiting to be called up to work. It will also depend on the time of day. All of this makes time more or less useable to support routines and choices around eating or exercising, seeing a doctor, resting, recovering, and the list goes on (Shove et al., 2009). Mothers typically combine their leisure and exercise with looking after children, so their time becomes more fragmented, less controllable and more easily disrupted. This also makes it harder to reap any health benefits (Mattingly & Blanchi, 2003). All of the dimensions of time draw on each other for their health impacts (Shove et al., 2009).

Even while time is a resource for health, its quality and value rests on its usability, and this is not reckoned just by hours and minutes.

Here I start with three premises about time as a socially shaped determinant of health. First, time is a resource people need for health. Second, time must be usable, that is, people must be able to direct it towards health, and this is where other aspects of time come into play. Third, not everyone has enough usable time for their health, as growing numbers of people lack 'spare' time that can be easily harnessed, redirected or used. Yet this lack of time is not random, it is, as I will explain in Chap. 3, deeply linked to our economic system and the unequal value placed on some types of time use (e.g. care vs paid employment) and some peoples' time over others. The problem of time for health does not fall evenly, and in this way, it is generating inequality as well as poorer health. Let me offer some ideas about how this works.

2.2 How Might Time Shape Health?

Tessa Grimmond and Amelia Yazidjoglou interviewed undergraduate university students who were working while they studied. They asked them how they made priorities, and what trade-offs they experienced and how they did (or didn't) find time for their health. Here is what they were told:

> Meals! I've given up a lot of meals. I've been trading off meals for sleep or showering... I'm not in a great financial position at the moment so I'm trying not to buy food out which means that I need to go home and cook but if I don't have time then I just end up not eating and pushing through. Having, like, a Pepsi or coffee. (Mary)

> Man, I would really - in an ideal world it would [be] uni, health, work (laughs). Um, but what it actually is, is: work, uni, then health. I don't have the time to make uni my priority. I don't have the financial ability to make uni my priority. And health just has to deal with it; you know? (Louise)

Oh! I. Can't. Afford to get sick! I can't afford to break a bone! That would just put my whole timeline on hold and that would make me probably get sick again from stress. (Tara)
   —Interviews with undergraduate university students who are working to support their study (Grimmond et al., 2020)

2.2.1 Compromise

It is not just good health that relies on time, everything people do needs time, like eating, resting, travelling, working, learning, consuming or caring for others. The problem is, there are 24 hours each day, so there is always a fixed limit, creating trade-offs when under pressure. These trade-offs affect health directly and indirectly. Mary gives up on meals, because she needs to put as much time as possible into earning money or studying, and a lack of both money and time compound her predicament. When the pressure is on, health is put last, as seen in Louise. Urgent needs like paying rent are put first. But, it's not just a one-way relationship between time and people's health. It is dynamic, and when people put health last, it will eventually be compromised. Then, illness, exhaustion or distress begins to affect what people can do. Unwell people can't use their time to do things like work or even study, a possibility Tara dreads. They lose jobs, sometimes relationships and then lose the resources that they bring.

2.2.2 Embodiment of Time

Nancy Krieger (2005) describes the way social circumstances and contexts alter minds and bodies through 'embodiment', an active process that connects things outside bodies to the biological and emotional things inside them. It is always complex and two-way, she calls it a web of influence. Time can become embodied (Krieger, 2014) through the requirements of jobs, care, study, travel or by the speed or slowness of effort, when and how much people do things, through deadlines and workloads that become worrying, overwhelming, exhausting or boring, and by creating trade-offs in other things that matter to health; 24/7 schedules desynchronise people from social interactions while also disrupting bio-logical and circadian rhythms, so the influence on health is multi-pronged (James et al., 2017; Täht & Mills, 2016). And when time is used as a social penalty (think of longer wait times or incarceration), it starts to drag people down. This means health and time almost certainly have more than one type of influence on each other. There is no single, right, wrong or even best way to think about how time and health affect each other, because there are multiple paths, with feedbacks and loops, and many of them join forces (actually, income affects health in similarly complex ways too, Marmot, 2002). What I offer in this book are six ways we could think about time and health connections—as a health hazard, a barrier, as a trade-off, through social weathering, exclusion (this is a reverse path) and a keystone for inequality.

2.3   Health Hazard

a source of danger
 to offer or present a risk
 (Merriam-Webster, 2020)

The standard approach in health is to view resources—like income—as a type of health hazard—a risk or exposure, whereby a certain amount, or not enough of it, causes harm. A medical example would be a toxic sub-stance like lead: the more a person is in contact or exposed to it, the greater the change in biology, and the more likely a health harm occurs. The exposure can be in reverse when things are good for people, like clean water or money, it's the lack that is harmful. Or there can be a 'sweet spot', calories are an example—too many or two few causing obesity or starvation. Time could be viewed as a social health hazard in a similar way, raising the question of whether there are demands on time that are too much, or too little, or if there is a 'sweet spot'. There have been decades of research that touches on this, estimating the impacts on health from underemployment (not enough hours) to long work hours and shift work, to name just two.

This is the approach most used in public health, so it is the first place I start. It's also where most of the evidence for time-health relationships can be found. This section focuses on research to date, far more than any of the other sections that follow it. My purpose is to underline the evidence base regarding time, without presenting an exhaustive review. A strength of this research is that it has actually thought about time well beyond a simple analysis of hours and minutes. Many different aspects of time show up—the amount of time (long hours), when time is free or constrained (mostly this is research on shift work), the ability to control time (usually this is covered by the term 'flexibility') and how the intensification of work linked to efficiency and technology might be altering well-being.

2.3.1 Hazardous Hours

"I enjoy walking and all that, but I don't do it that often because I'm just knackered all the time" (Blue-collar male working 11–12-hour days) (Dixon et al., 2019). The aspect of time which has likely gained the most attention has been the length of time spent working. Long work hours (usually defined as 50 hours a week or more) predict health problems such as cardiovascular disease, diabetes and depression. They change biological markers that precede disease (such as blood pressure changes, or poor immunological function) as well as exercise and healthy eating, as that quote above describes (Devine et al., 2009; Dixon et al., 2019; Van der Hulst, 2003). Long work hours create what is called a sleep debt, and they make people tired as the worker describes above (Kageyama et al., 2001; Kageyama et al., 1998). Not all studies agree on how long work hours need to be before they become hazardous. Most show that as work hours increase so does the impact on health (Artazcoz et al., 2009). Our research shows that the hazard depends on the other demands on people's time (Dinh et al., 2017). Huong Dinh's analysis of 5 years of data showed that (like the example of calories) working is good for most people up to a point. This is not surprising given all the benefits having a job delivers, but after that point—39 hours—each additional hour worked risks harming mental health.

2.3.2 Hazardous Schedules

When people's work can be hazardous, this line of research on time and health has revealed how important timing, synchrony and predictability are (Knutsson, 2003). In the US, a third of the workforce works weekends and over a quarter work from late night to early morning (Hamermesh & Stancanelli, 2015). In the UK it's fairly similar, with over one quarter working weekends and one fifth working the late-night shift. It varies across countries; in Germany and France the percentage working weekends or late at night is somewhat lower. Either way, however, large groups of people around the world are working at unsociable times. The most clear-cut is shift work—jobs during the evenings or night—or with schedules that change and rotate. People who work these unsociable times tend to exercise less (Atkinson et al., 2008) and sleep less, with sleep debts of between 1 and 4 hours every day (Niu et al., 2011). As well as circadian disruption there are digestive disruptions—they eat more junk food and calories, which then set up a cascade of health harms including type 2 diabetes (Esquirol et al., 2009; Pan et al., 2011; Tada et al., 2014; Van Drongelen et al., 2011). Timing is important beyond bodily rhythms because social connections require synchronising too. Divorce is more common (Presser, 2000), and depression increases. One shift worker interviewed by Jane Dixon and Lara Corr described how this happens; "Sometimes it could be, like, four days that I won't see my family at all, which means that all the work and stress is on my wife, because she has to get the kids ready for school, bathe, cook, dress them, get them ready for bed, and put up with all the stresses of children" (unpublished interview, Jane Dixon and Lara Corr, "Contestations over work time: Should health weigh in?"). What this man describes is a daily disruption to his relationships, since his 'free' time wasn't socially usable (Strazdins et al., 2006).

2.3.3 Lack of Control or Flexibility

It wasn't that long ago that time punches were a feature of workplaces. You might have seen them in the movies. People would queue up and enter a card into a punch which stamped on it exactly when they started or stopped work. This is not very common these days, although there are other forms of checking when people begin or end work, such as digital fingerprints and logins. What punch cards reflect is rigid and inflexible work time, whereby people are monitored and penalised if they don't comply. It hasn't gone entirely, inflexible time is still widespread in manufacturing and service jobs, but as the knowledge economy grows, the numbers of workers who are privileged and can change their start and stop times have risen.

Having control and flexibility with time is obviously important for anyone whose time outside of work is constrained by study or care and so it is likely to deliver health benefits (Costa et al., 2006). It's easy to imagine how being able to fit time for health around time for work and vice versa would lower the costs and barriers to exercise, good sleep, the ability to shop and cook healthy food or even seeing a doctor for anyone (Devine et al., 2003; Grzywacz et al., 2007). It may not give extra hours and minutes, but having control and flexibility increases the usability of time. As one mother explained in Ginny Sargent's study of work time and health routines, "I would have probably had to quit my job ... that flexibility has been so fantastic. So, yeah, it's so important for people, especially once they have kids, you just don't have time, you need some give" (Sargent et al., 2018).

2.3.4 Intensification

Intensity is about how hard and fast people work (see Chap. 1). It is linked to technology, which delivers tasks immediately—and creates the expectation to respond immediately. This makes it difficult for managers or workers to discern how much work they need to do, or how fast they can and should do it, but it's not simply a problem for digitally delivered work. As one manufacturing study argued, the speed of production lines could be doubled; the only limit is human (Allwood et al., 2016).

Working fast, often without breaks, trying to squeeze and compress time and fit more and more in is, to some extent, a logical response to efficiency. The problem is, no one knows where to draw the line, and in the absence of any standards, the pressure to keep doing more continues. There is good evidence that this is a health hazard. Having a sustained, fast and pressured work pace is consistently linked to fatigue, exhaustion, stress, burn out, musculoskeletal injuries and poorer work-life balance (Boxall & Macky, 2014; Macky & Boxall, 2008; Zoer et al., 2011). Mental health, including depression and anxiety, is also another casualty (Airila et al., 2014; Boxall & Macky, 2014; Macky & Boxall, 2008; Moen et al., 2013; Murcia et al., 2013; Stansfeld et al., 1995; Volkoff et al., 2010; Zoer et al., 2011). Even small reductions in pace and pressure lead to better energy and self-assessed health, less exhaustion and less distress (Moen et al., 2013).

Technology is not the only source of work intensity. Sometimes the 'people' demands of the job are hard to fit within a strict time limit (which is often what must be done). This is particularly true of work which involves helping or serving. In Australia, general practitioner physicians are paid for every 15 minutes of consultation. This is barely enough time to understand what the problem is, particularly if there are several. Yet every patient is booked into 15-minute appointments, so the responsibility is on a doctor to work within it—and this pressure is hazardous to both doctors and patients. As a general practitioner said, "that's a huge pressure …. You know people so rarely come in with one problem … some days I just find that absolutely exhausting. You know everybody has at least three problems and want you to get it all done in 15 minutes" (E. Strazdins et al., 2019).

To take stock, there is plenty of evidence for my argument that time is important to health. Certainly the evidence is there for hours, flexibility and control, scheduling and intensity. Framing time as a workplace health hazard meshes with the long tradition and acceptance of other workplace health hazards (exposures to chemical toxins, injuries, physical strains).

While important, and sympathetic to how public health has often investigated social determinants, a hazard approach is in my view incomplete. It lacks clarity on how time joins forces with power to shape health and misses the way it shapes inequity. It also tries to isolate which aspects are hazardous, testing various dimensions of time such as the number of hours, timing, intensity and control. There has been no higher-order articulation of a time-and-health agenda as a consequence. Almost no one has pulled the various dimensions of time together; one notable exception is health sociologist Jane Dixon, whose interviews with managers and workers show how the different dimensions of work time (predictability, flexibility, amount, synchrony) interlock to harm health by altering eating, sleeping, social relationships, and exercise (Boivin et al., 2007; Dixon et al., 2019).

2.4 Barrier

a structure that prevents or hinders movement or action
   something immaterial that impedes or separates
   (Merriam-Webster, 2020)

Another way to think about the way time affects health is to view it as a cost that some people can't afford. This is what people mean when they say they're too busy to exercise or eat healthy food. They are talking about the way time acts as a barrier, it is too high a price for them to pay, especially if there are money costs as well, as Danielle Venn (Venn & Strazdins, 2017) shows. In her analysis of 5000 people over 3 years she followed people whose income or time reduced to put them into a relatively 'poor' category. They were all healthy. Dr Venn was testing behaviour change; she wanted to know what happens when otherwise healthy people, without significant time or income scarcity to start with, faced a change in their social circumstance. She found that a lowering of their income shifted about 5% of otherwise healthy people into inactivity. The same thing happened with a reduction in free time, due to either care or work, or both increasing. One in ten faced a constraint in both time and money, and this doubled the rate of behaviour change. She considered time inside and outside work (a major innovation), so it included care, travel and so on, giving the first longitudinal evidence that time scarcity is a barrier to health.

2.4.1 Opportunity Costs

A strength of the cost or barrier framework is it aligns with an explicit (and politically favoured) economic frame. It positions time costs as opportunity costs that change individual behaviour (which is what public health tries to do with its health messaging). Every business and marketer knows this. Saving time improves consumption and sales. Advertisements aggressively market to time poor consumers, offering them quicker, simpler and easier products and services (and ways to purchase them). Time sells. People buy fast and processed food because it is quick. It saves time (Rydell et al., 2008). Now, Uber Eats and Deliveroo offer further time savings on travel, which is another way to increase sales. Ironically, public health could learn a lot about time from the success of the fast-food industry.

The cost is not just sparing hours or minutes, there are opportunity costs for other potential uses of time. These costs are often calculated in terms of what they're stopping people from doing, and how this is valued relative to health. Ginny Sargent and Cathy Banwell studied why health promotion was absent or rarely used in some workplaces. They interviewed a range of businesses, big and small. Here is what one manager of a smaller enterprise told them. His employee's time spent on work tasks was carefully maximised. In fact, it was considered so valuable that the cost of freeing up time during work hours (which embeds time and money costs) was an insurmountable barrier to offering exercise programmes. He said, "We work here in five minute blocks, so every five minutes we spend doing something in this organisation is counted…. if they want to do something … they've got their hour lunch break, we don't want them extending it. We don't want it impacting on work…. [this environment] supports the more soft stuff like the weekends, the fruit, and the occasional visit by someone talking about health and safety issues" (Sargent et al., 2018).

This quote reveals the economic value of time, and its ability to act as a disincentive even when you control it (as the manager controls employee time). These workplaces even said they would rather give their staff money (such as $100 to buy a gym membership) or spend money (buy fruit or standing desks) than allocate them an extra 30 minutes for health during the work day (Sargent et al., 2018).

2.4.2 Relational Costs

The costs can also be impacts on others, and they can be emotional and relational (not just financial). Kaye Mentha interviewed employed mothers about how they manage to feed their families healthy food (Mehta et al., 2020). One mother explains why she sometimes serves fast food to her family. "[my two year old] falls asleep in the car on the way home and I've got no opportunity to get in food, so um, on those, occasionally I end up resorting to fast food [be]cause there doesn't feel to me like there's much option. Absolutely right, fast food for me is convenience and a necessity on occasion, or it feels like a necessity, I'm sure I have different choices but it is an option that is quick." She wants to make meals faster (because she is time-poor), but she doesn't want to wake her son (he may become distressed and needs his sleep) and can't leave him to shop for healthy ingredients. She frames the choice for fast food as a necessity but a last resort, a way of trying to reconcile her deeply felt responsibility to cook healthy food despite its high costs.

A second mother explained "it would be nice if you had plenty of time to do you know, if it wasn't such a chore you know, wouldn't make you so tired when you were doing it and you get to the point where you can't think, I can't think what am I going to have tomorrow night for tea, let alone tonight. So, I can't think ahead because there's too much going on … I can't bear the thought of cooking, I think I'm just so tired." The feeling of having to do more incurs a cost, which can be overwhelming and exhausting (a line of influence joining mental and physical health). All the mothers interviewed were aware of the need for healthy food and felt a moral responsibility to deliver it, but in the face of so much going on, with no easy way to find the time, it felt like an insurmountable demand—an unbearable cost on them.

When resources become scarce (either time or money), any additional 'spend' is viewed differently. It is seen as having a greater cost that it would if the time or money required was plentiful. The more that time gets filled up, maximised and used, the costlier (or greater barrier) time for health becomes. Once you think about time as a barrier, it raises questions about for whom it is the costliest and why. And this brings me to the notion of trade-offs. Trade-offs are another way to think about how time and health are connected. A trade-off perspective is helpful because it considers not only what people are doing with their time but what they are not. This raises issues of choice, power and usability. It turns a light onto what people don't or can't do, and asks why. It takes the ideas of hazard, cost and barrier and places them within the explicit acknowledgement that there is a system every person works within, that is subject to a 24-hour limit.

2.5   Trade-off

A balancing of factors all of which are not attainable at the same time
A giving up of one thing in return for another
(Merriam-Webster, 2020)

Mary and Louise (the university students from earlier in this chapter) reveal how trade-offs work, and how easy it is for health to lose out. Mary gives up on meals because she is trading off her time to make money, and because the interplay between lack of money and lack of time means she can't afford to buy healthy food *and* she doesn't have the time to cook it. The trade-off is also the source of, and doubles, the disincentive.

Louise highlights the vulnerability of health to more urgent trade-offs. She needs to use her time to earn enough money to meet her bills, that's her most urgent priority. She also needs to use her time to study, trusting that it will help secure money and a career in the future. Her health fades into the background as the last priority. It has the least immediate and longest-term consequence, making it less urgent, more dismissible, easier to give up or at least cut back. The problem is that Louise and Mary are not alone in putting their health last. Sixty-four per cent of US men and 35% of US women aged 21–64 years spend no time in daily food preparation at all (Jabs & Devine, 2006). Only one half of adult Americans or Australians meet the minimum of 30 minutes for physical activity (CDC, 2018).

There is a clear limit on anyone's time—24 hours every day. This sets the parameter for how much people can do. Each extra demand on time may not seem like much, but for every extra minute or hour needed to fill out an online form, access a service, wait in a queue, answer an email or traverse a sprawling or poorly serviced city takes time from some other activity, and can make time less usable. That is not a major problem when other demands are low, but it ramps up once the need for time increases, so the problem can affect many people. This is what generates trade-offs that lock people into poverty and out of equality. Girls in sub-Saharan Africa walk an average of 6 miles every day to fetch water, which prevents them getting an education. This trade-off locks them out, not just one girl, or even one thousand, but millions (Reid, Walk for water: you 6K vs. theirs). It is what Melinda Gates meant when she says "What amazing goals would you accomplish with an extra hour every day? Or, in the case of girls in many poor countries, an extra five or more?" (Gates & Gates, 2016). Sometimes health itself is what gets given up and prioritised last. The 24-hour limit is unique to time, and the fact that any activity has to take time from something else underlies almost all of the ways that time shapes health. It is why work time can be hazardous, and it is why time is such a powerful disincentive once it becomes scarce. It is the process through which a lack of time locks in a lack of income, and both of these then compromise health (ACOSS, 2018; Burchardt, 2008). Here is an example.

2.5.1 Poverty

In the US, millions of people live on or below the poverty line (currently 38 million) (Semega et al., 2017). Many of them can't afford fresh food, and their nutritional outcomes, especially among children, are universally alarming. In response, the US government, who provides food stamps, developed a Thrifty Food Plan to improve health. The intention was to direct food stamps towards buying and eating fresh, unprocessed and healthy food using a 'cook from scratch approach'. Food stamps were tied to certain ingredients (legumes, fresh vegetables, etc.), so that food needed to be made at home. The problem was that this took a lot more time to do. It took 16 hours every week or nearly 2½ hours every day to prepare food from scratch for a family of four. This was well ahead of the time spent by most women (rich or poor) in the US, even those who were not employed. Yet more than a third of food stamp households were single parents (mostly mothers) and many held jobs too. These income-poor mothers were also profoundly time-poor, a problem health policy didn't see. The Plan added to these mothers' burdens, forcing them to make trade-offs between their time at work or time preparing food, or even the time they could spend with their children. Because of this, many households couldn't meet the nutritional standards, and the most important reason was lack of time (Davis & You, 2011; Rose, 2007).

2.5.2 Wealth

An interesting thing about the lack of usable time is that it can create trade-offs right across the socio-economic spectrum. It challenges the way we think about disadvantage and could broaden how we define it. Certainly, it is a problem for the income-poor or low-skilled because their time earns them far less money. But even the well-to-do can face time trade-offs. They are a constant possibility for anyone who has significant demands that are difficult to control or delegate. Thus, women's invisible and devalued care time feminises poverty, but time constraint can be a problem for anyone, male, female or non-binary who shoulder unpaid work whether they are a manager or on welfare, inequity in time runs right across the socio-economic spectrum once care creates trade-offs with earning income. Many people who work long hours earn good money. They are educated and may have come from privileged families. But even if there is no barrier from lack of money (or education, or even expertise about the importance of healthy behaviour) they can still face time trade-offs that compromise health. Consider the Australian GPs (men and women) interviewed by Kathryn Dwan and Erika Strazdins (E. Strazdins et al., 2019). They were, by anyone's measure, well paid and well educated. But, they still suffered acutely from time scarcity. They described being unable to take time off from work when they were ill, having nervous breakdowns, of struggling both professionally and ethically with the pressure of providing quality health care when working under such strict and overwhelming time limits. Their time pressure meant that they faced trade-offs between earning income (if they reduced the number of patients they saw), their own health (if they rushed or worked longer hours) or the quality of care they provided patients (if they stuck to the strict 15-minute deadline). Yet, they were otherwise considered high status and well resourced.

There are other ways that time shapes health, though, that rest much more openly on the connections between time and power. Time can also be used to punish, discriminate and exclude people in ways that affect health, through a process of social weathering.

2.6   Social Weathering

The action of weather [social] conditions in altering the colour, texture, composition or form of exposed objects
(Merriam-Webster, 2020)

Social weathering describes the repeated experience of social and economic marginalisation and how it changes health (Geronimus et al., 2006). This idea evokes the way climate and natural forces wear down objects, leading to premature ageing. It is a term that has been used to describe the experience of daily racism and health inequality but can equally be applied to almost all marginalised groups. It explains how constant stress (sometimes called allostatic load (McEwen & Seeman, 1999)) changes emotions, physiology and neurotransmitters, and alters neuroendocrine processes and immune functioning, all of which ages and erodes bodies and minds. It's the way discrimination gets embodied, both the subtle and not-so-subtle slights, dismissals or outright abuses that people of colour, women, welfare recipients, particular religious groupings, diverse genders and non-binary, or the disabled suffer almost every single day. Their body and their mind are weathered by social processes; it changes biology but is not due to biology, it is due to the way they are treated.

2.6.1 Socioeconomic Disadvantage

Imagine a single parent with two small children. She is poor, she doesn't have a job and she relies on government welfare. Every month she checks in with her caseworker. She first completes forms about her expenditure online, submits them and makes an appointment. She is given a time and date. She arrives with her children in a stroller, and the room is full of others waiting for their appointments too. She gets in a queue, registers and sits down to wait. Nearly an hour passes. It's hard to amuse the children, and it's noisy. It becomes well past her allotted time, and one of the children needs to go to the toilet. But there is no toilet nearby. She needs to go across the road to the shopping mall, and when she returns her number has been called, and she's missed her appointment. She gets in another queue to try to solve this problem. She waits her turn. The staff understand but there is nothing they can do. So, she travels back home on two buses, logs on again, makes another appointment, and then comes back another day.

This was an account given at a public health conference of the way that government systems, especially online systems, reinforce socioeconomic disadvantage. As I listened, what became interesting to me was the way time was used as a social tool. It wasn't simply the realisation that government cost cutting meant services now lacked toilets, it was the way this welfare recipient's time was penalised. The system controlled the time (not even the staff could change the list), it was part of the quid pro quo for receiving a benefit (a welfare version of a wage–time exchange, except in this case time is handed over for benefits). There was no flexibility, and very little predictability. There were long waits and time-consuming tasks required to navigate the system, and this was all repeated every month. She faced a deep time cost embedded in the trip, the waits, accessing amenities and then starting all over again. Her time wasn't valued or visible. In fact, the whole system treated her time as expendable—and, in a system where welfare recipients were treated as flawed, lazy or parasitic, these time costs formed part of the 'disincentive'. It was assumed that if she is not working, she has nothing better to do, which effectively erased how such time costs were acting to make her life harder.

2.6.2 Time for Health Care

Low income joins forces with time in social weathering, for example, health care waiting times. In Australia, people on the lowest income are two to three times more likely to smoke, have diabetes, be unable to pay for a dentist, or medication, and to die of potentially avoidable disease (AIHW, 2018). But they are also more likely to have a long wait for health care—a 65% longer wait. For short wait procedures in hospitals this translates to about 2 days longer wait for those at the bottom of the income ladder compared to those at the top. But for procedures that generally have long waiting times such as elective surgery, it can make a 4-month difference (Johar et al., 2013). Quite a significant time penalty. Julian Hart describes this as the inverse care law, whereby the availability of health care varies inversely with the need for it among people (Hart, 1971). Thus, marginalised people often have the poorest health (through social weathering) and then face a further time and health cost, waiting longer in hospitals for surgery. They travel further to access services (in the US, Blacks and Hispanics spend 10 minutes longer each way (Carr et al., 2010). They then wait longer in hospitals, and this time penalty is not just confined to marginalised adults who seek health care, it also extends to their children (Park et al., 2009; Pell et al., 2000). For some, such as Blacks and Hispanics in the US, this totals to a 25–28% additional time burden every time they see the doctor (Ray et al., 2015).

Gilbert Gee and his colleagues describe how time is weathering African-Americans in the US, who wait longer to be served and to access services, even to cross a road, and they are also given longer terms in jail. It is not just in the US of course. Indigenous Australians wait longer than other Australians for elective surgery (AIHW, 2018). Women in pain are less likely to be treated, or have their pain rated in the same ways men are (Hoffmann & Tarzian, 2001). Time is used in the process of weathering, linked partly to assumptions that anyone who is income-poor is time-rich. This is not the whole story. It is also linked to the different value given to people's time based on their social status. The result is constant, repeated stress that is uncontrollable and pervasive, affecting health through allostatic load. And when time is 'lost' or penalised, it creates an opportunity cost—it stops people from doing something else. The single mother in my example could not use her 3 or 4 hours of waiting and travel to exercise, rest, or prepare nutritious food. This forms another loop back to health.

2.7 Exclusion

To prevent or restrict entrance
To bar from participation, consideration or inclusion
(Merriam-Webster, 2020)

Lack of income erodes health, because it deprives people of the opportunities as well as material resources they need to be healthy. It is an obvious pathway. Actually though, the relationship is complex and dynamic and operates equally in the reverse. People with poor health are less able to work, and when they do work, they work fewer hours and earn less money. This means bad health also pulls people down and reduces their ability to earn income. This makes the relationship between income and health a two-way process which then becomes a downward spiral. A similar reverse influence happens with time—it runs from health to time. Here is an example.

People with kidney failure need to undertake time-consuming dialysis and health care regimes. This usually means travelling to a clinic or hospital, plus a hard-to-predict wait for their service. The time costs of their health care pose a problem for anyone who has a job. The people Julia McQuoid (2015) interviewed described waiting, often for hours, for the dialysis machine, having left work to do so. Sometimes they also needed to get a prescription and would then make an additional appointment, travel, wait, get the prescription, then get it filled (another wait) before they could go back to work. The treatment itself took many hours. A few of the people she interviewed had flexible jobs and were well paid and valuable employees. They took their computers, working in the waiting rooms or as they lay on the dialysis bed. But some, such as the man who delivered mail, or the chef who worked long hours through evenings and nights, simply couldn't move their worktime around their health, or do both things at once. They had quit their jobs and become unemployed, losing income as well as self-identity. In a time-use survey, these people would look like they had 'free time', but their health caused it. It was not free time that they chose, nor was it easily usable. Their health excluded them, partly through its time burden.

2.7.1 Opportunities Lost to Health

Poor health—mental illness, disability, and most health conditions—dramatically reduces people's opportunity to gain and keep jobs (and other things such as travel, attend school or university). Poor health is the main reason people leave the labour market or retire early (OECD & European Union, 2016; Roberts et al., 2010). Exclusion on the basis of health is rarely conceptualised as a form of discrimination. It is so normal, acceptable and well-established that it is neither remarkable nor considered a social problem (West & Hepworth, 1991). This 'excluding' quality of poor health affects people's ability to do many things, which means it alters how people can use their time. Long hours are not possible to sustain, even for the healthy, but the short-hour jobs offer lower status and lower pay (Pagán, 2013). Poor health and disability locks people out of resources like income, education or feeling valued—economists have known this for decades. Health is an input to productivity and labour market success (a key part of human capital) and not just a result of it.

Health exclusion takes social weathering a further step because it makes explicit that time and health have a two-way relationship. Thus, longer waits and every-day extra time costs erode health, but the opposite is also true: when people's health is eroded, they redirect time to their health (resting, medical appointments) and reduce demands because they are either physically or mentally unable to cope with them. They 'drift down' and these two-way relationships between health and time create downward or upward spirals.

This is the reverse relationship I mentioned at the beginning of this chapter. It's where health drives how people use their time and not vice versa. In a society that places a premium on efficiency, where people are recruited and advanced because they can work long and fast, it's easy to see how time plays a part—it's survival of the fastest. This interplay between time affecting health, and health altering how people use their time is an important one to grasp, because research on time and health cannot assume a linear relationship. Lots of free time is associated with worse health outcomes. But this is not because 'free time' is bad for health (and being busy is good), it might mean people are already ill or unhealthy, and so have been excluded from jobs or care-giving. Healthy people in contrast can use their time fully. Up to a point, being busy is good for people, unless they neglect time for their health. Then there is a limit. The fact that people's health affects their time reveals an important (albeit opposite) way society is shaping health. It's what university student Tara meant when she said she couldn't afford to get sick.

2.8 Inequity Keystone

Unjust or unfair
   piece at the crown of the arch that locks the other pieces in place
   (Merriam-Webster, 2020)

I, like many health scholars, have pictured poor health as a 'result' of social inequity and lack of income. But what if it is more like a system, where the pieces of the system lock each other into place? And, what if the pieces are not just money and the resources money buys, but includes time, because time is needed to earn income *and* needed for health? Each element relies on the other to lock inequity in. This is what I mean by the word 'keystone'. A time-money-health system which keeps the inequity structure rigid. Where people start in terms of their money, time or health, and where they can go, is intimately tied to this dynamic. It is not just money. It's not just time. It is not just health. It is the interplay, and time helps lock it into place.

Let me explain. Time *is* money, in the sense that you need time to earn income (in the absence of any other wealth). But, if you accept my argument that time is a resource people need for health this straightaway makes for tension between how much time can be used to earn money (which is the key marker of inequality in our society) and the trade-off this creates with time available for health. This is an absolute trade-off, because there are only 24 hours every day. Some of our time must be used for health, even in the short term to meet basic needs (to sleep, eat, take medications, etc.) but to really protect health, time each day is required for regular exercise and eating healthy food. It is impossible to go past the 24-hour time limit, so your only option is to cut time needed for health, or time needed to earn income.

The health trade-off creates a limit to people's options to work their way out of poverty or inequality, no matter how much they try. But, this hasn't been clearly articulated in most analyses of social inequality. Largely, social inequality is seen as the downward driving force on health. It starts from a lack of resources, either due to resource gaps in childhood (born in a poor family, poor quality education) or to a lack of opportunity later in life (job loss, industry risk restructuring, etc.). Where health comes into it, it's either seen as an output (people's health deteriorates because they don't have enough money, good housing, etc.) or perhaps also as an input (poor health then compromises people's life chances, especially over the life course and generates social exclusion, this is termed 'health selection').

But health takes both an output and input place in this process because of its relationship with time. If you are poor and work in a low-wage job and you want to increase your income, your best option is to increase your hours (maybe work more shifts at unsociable times or take a second or third job). But there are only so many more hours you can work before your health will be harmed. Even if you push through for a few months, or perhaps a year, once you harm your health, you compromise your ability to keep working and damage your productivity. You hit a time *and* health ceiling. You are stuck with the options of continuing to harm your health or cut back your hours (or jobs) and therefore earnings to protect your health. Either way it makes for a lose-lose.

2.8.1 Time-Money-Health System

Marx understood this time-money-health system long before it dawned on others. He wrote: "the occupation....is made by mere excess the destroyer of man. He can strike so many blows per day, walk so many steps, breathe so many breaths produce so much work, and live an average, say of fifty years; he is made to strike so many more blows, to walk so many more steps, to breathe so many more breaths per day, and to increase altogether a fourth of his life. He meets the effort; the result is, that producing for a limited time a fourth more work, he dies at 37 for 50" (Tucker et al., 1978, p. 372). He was, however, literally talking about men. His analysis of health, time and money trade-offs as integral to power relationships completely missed women's (or any caregiver's) time. He only thought about paid work, no other time entered his analysis. Because of this, it's been far too easy to focus on money as the wellspring of power and inequity and forget the extra part played by time (Nyland, 1990).

But what if your time earns no money (despite its value)? The time I'm referring to is the time every society (and economy) relies on, and that is the time needed to raise children, cook the meals, clean, run errands, the list goes on. It is necessary time not just within households, but to the renewal of the whole society. So, if your time is not counted economically (and this time isn't), if it doesn't earn you money, then it further compromises your opportunity to earn your way out of poverty, or protect time for health. Marx missed this critical point. He saw that the power relationships pivoted on the wage–time exchange in the market. He missed that time outside the market was equally important to power and to health. This keystone idea draws on time (and money) as health hazards but puts them within a system of trade-offs and barriers that dictate people's opportunity. Health is an input and an output, as are all the social resources. It is in my view a key element to gender inequality, class inequity and generational inequity, all of which are inseparable from health inequity. It's complex, it sounds messy, it is what Nancy Krieger was referring to when she described the causal web. She was describing a system that locks in racism. What I want to do is explore it further, focusing on the gender and generational dimensions, in the next chapter.

References

ACOSS. (2018). *Poverty in Australia*. Australian Council of Social Service and University of New South Wales.

AIHW. (2018). *Australia's health 2018*. Australian Institute of Health and Welfare.

Airila, A., Hakanen, J. J., Luukkonen, R., Lusa, S., Punakallio, A., & Leino-Arjas, P. (2014). Developmental trajectories of multisite musculoskeletal pain and depressive symptoms: The effects of job demands and resources and individual factors. *Psychology & Health, 29*(12), 1421–1441.

Allwood, J. M., Childs, T. H., Clare, A. T., De Silva, A. K., Dhokia, V., Hutchings, I. M., et al. (2016). Manufacturing at double the speed. *Journal of Materials Processing Technology, 229*, 729–757.

Artazcoz, L., Cortès, I., Escribà-Agüir, V., Cascant, L., & Villegas, R. (2009). Understanding the relationship of long working hours with health status and health-related behaviours. *Journal of Epidemiology & Community Health, 63*(7), 521–527.

Atkinson, G., Fullick, S., Grindey, C., & Maclaren, D. (2008). Exercise, energy balance and the shift worker. *Sports Medicine, 38*(8), 671–685.

Boivin, D. B., Tremblay, G. M., & James, F. O. (2007). Working on atypical schedules. *Sleep Medicine, 8*(6), 578–589. https://doi.org/10.1016/j.sleep.2007.03.015

Boxall, P., & Macky, K. (2014). High-involvement work processes, work intensification and employee well-being. *Work, Employment and Society, 28*(6), 963–984.

Burchardt, T. (2008). *Time and income poverty. CASE report 57*. Centre for Analysis of Social Exclusion London School of Economics: Joseph Rountree Foundation.

Carr, D., Ibuka, Y., & Russell, L. B. (2010). How much time do Americans spend seeking health care? Racial and ethnic differences in patient experiences. In *The impact of demographics on health and health care: Race, ethnicity and other social factors*. Emerald Group Publishing Limited.

CDC. (2018). *Trends in meeting the 2008 physical activity guidelines, 2008—2018*. Centers for Disease Control and Prevention.

Costa, G., Sartori, S., & Åkerstedt, T. (2006). Influence of flexibility and variability of working hours on health and well-being. *Chronobiology International, 23*(6), 1125–1137.

Davis, G. C., & You, W. (2011). Not enough money or not enough time to satisfy the Thrifty Food Plan? A cost difference approach for estimating a money–time threshold. *Food Policy, 36*(2), 101–107.

Devine, C. M., Connors, M. M., Sobal, J., & Bisogni, C. A. (2003). Sandwiching it in: Spillover of work onto food choices and family roles in low-and moderate-income urban households. *Social Science & Medicine, 56*(3), 617–630.

Devine, C. M., Farrell, T. J., Blake, C. E., Jastran, M., Wethington, E., & Bisogni, C. A. (2009). Work conditions and the food choice coping strategies of employed parents. *Journal of Nutrition Education and Behavior, 41*(5), 365–370.

Dinh, H., Strazdins, L., & Welsh, J. (2017). Hour-glass ceilings: Work-hour thresholds, gendered health inequities. *Social Science & Medicine, 176*, 42–51.

Dixon, J., Banwell, C., Strazdins, L., Corr, L., & Burgess, J. (2019). Flexible employment policies, temporal control and health promoting practices: A qualitative study in two Australian worksites. *PLoS One, 14*, e0224542. https://doi.org/10.1371/journal.pone.0224542

Dunstan, D., Barr, E., Healy, G., Salmon, J., Shaw, J., Balkau, B., et al. (2010). Television viewing time and mortality: The Australian diabetes, obesity and lifestyle study (AusDiab). *Circulation, 121*(3), 384.

Esquirol, Y., Bongard, V., Mabile, L., Jonnier, B., Soulat, J. M., & Perret, B. (2009). Shift work and metabolic syndrome: Respective impacts of job strain, physical activity, and dietary rhythms. *Chronobiology International, 26*(3), 544–559.

Gates, B., & Gates, M. (2016). *Two superpowers we wish we had: Melinda and I want more time and energy—For everyone.* https://www.gatesnotes.com/2016-Annual-Letter

Geronimus, A. T., Hicken, M., Keene, D., & Bound, J. (2006). "Weathering" and age patterns of allostatic load scores among blacks and whites in the United States. *American Journal of Public Health, 96*(5), 826–833.

Grimmond, T., Yazidjoglou, A., & Strazdins, L. (2020). Earning to learn: The time-health trade-offs of employed Australian undergraduate students. *Health Promotion International, 35*(6), 1302–1311. https://doi.org/10.1093/heapro/daz133

Grzywacz, J. G., Casey, P. R., & Jones, F. A. (2007). The effects of workplace flexibility on health behaviors: A cross-sectional and longitudinal analysis. *Journal of Occupational and Environmental Medicine, 49*(12), 1302–1309.

Hamermesh, D. S., & Stancanelli, E. (2015). Long workweeks and strange hours. *ILR Review, 68*(5), 1007–1018.

Hart, J. T. (1971). The inverse care law. *The Lancet, 297*(7696), 405–412.

Hoffmann, D. E., & Tarzian, A. J. (2001). The girl who cried pain: A bias against women in the treatment of pain. *The Journal of Law, Medicine & Ethics, 28*, 13–27.

Hu, F. B., Li, T. Y., Colditz, G. A., Willett, W. C., & Manson, J. E. (2003). Television watching and other sedentary behaviors in relation to risk of obesity and type 2 diabetes mellitus in women. *JAMA, 289*(14), 1785–1791.

Jabs, J., & Devine, C. M. (2006). Time scarcity and food choices: An overview. *Appetite, 47*(2), 196–204.

James, S. M., Honn, K. A., Gaddameedhi, S., & Van Dongen, H. P. (2017). Shift work: Disrupted circadian rhythms and sleep—Implications for health and well-being. *Current Sleep Medicine Reports, 3*(2), 104–112.

Johar, M., Jones, G., Keane, M., Savage, E., & Stavrunova, O. (2013). Discrimination in a universal health system: Explaining socioeconomic waiting time gaps. *Journal of Health Economics, 32*(1), 181–194.

Kageyama, T., Nishikido, N., Kobayashi, T., & Kawagoe, H. (2001). Estimated sleep debt and work stress in Japanese white-collar workers. *Psychiatry and Clinical Neurosciences, 55*(3), 217–219.

Kageyama, T., Nishikido, N., Kobayashi, T., Kurokawa, Y., Kaneko, T., & Kabuto, M. (1998). Long commuting time, extensive overtime, and sympathodominant state assessed in terms of short-term heart rate variability among male white-collar workers in the Tokyo megalopolis. *Industrial Health, 36*(3), 209–217.

Knutsson, A. (2003). Health disorders of shift workers. *Occupational Medicine, 53*(2), 103–108.

Krantz-Kent, R. (2018). Television, capturing America's attention at prime time and beyond. *Beyond the Numbers: Special Studies and Research, 7*, 14.

Krieger, N. (2005). Embodiment: A conceptual glossary for epidemiology. *Journal of Epidemiology and Community Health, 59*(5), 350–355. https://doi.org/10.1136/jech.2004.024562

Krieger, N. (2014). Got Theory? On the 21st c. CE rise of explicit use of epidemiologic theories of disease distribution: A review and ecosocial analysis. *Current Epidemiology Reports, 1*(1), 45–56.

Macky, K., & Boxall, P. (2008). High-involvement work processes, work intensification and employee well-being: A study of New Zealand worker experiences. *Asia Pacific Journal of Human Resources, 46*(1), 38–55.

Marmot, M. (2002). The influence of income on health: Views of an epidemiologist. *Health Affairs, 21*(2), 31–46.

Mattingly, M. J., & Blanchi, S. M. (2003). Gender differences in the quantity and quality of free time: The US experience. *Social Forces, 81*(3), 999–1030.

McEwen, B. S., & Seeman, T. (1999). Protective and damaging effects of mediators of stress. Elaborating and testing the concepts of allostasis and allostatic load. *Annals N Y Academy of Science, 896*, 30–47. https://doi.org/10.1111/j.1749-6632.1999.tb08103.x

McQuoid, J., Welsh, J., Strazdins, L., Griffin, A., & Banwell, C. (2015). Integrating paid work and chronic illness in daily life: A space-time approach to understanding the challenges. *Health and Place, 34*, 83–91. https://doi.org/10.1016/j.healthplace.2015.04.001

Mehta, K., Booth, S., Coveney, J., & Strazdins, L. (2020). Feeding the Australian family: Challenges for mothers, nutrition and equity. *Health Promotion International, 35*(4), 771–778. https://doi.org/10.1093/heapro/daz061

Merriam-Webster. (2020). https://www.merriam-webster.com/dictionary/trade-off

Moen, P., Kelly, E. L., & Lam, J. (2013). Healthy work revisited: Do changes in time strain predict well-being? *Journal of Occupational Health Psychology, 18*(2), 157–172.

Murcia, M., Chastang, J.-F., & Niedhammer, I. (2013). Psychosocial work factors, major depressive and generalised anxiety disorders: Results from the French national SIP study. *Journal of Affective Disorders, 146*(3), 319–327.

Niu, S.-F., Chung, M.-H., Chen, C.-H., Hegney, D., O'Brien, A., & Chou, K.-R. (2011). The effect of shift rotation on employee cortisol profile, sleep quality, fatigue, and attention level: A systematic review. *Journal of Nursing Research, 19*(1), 68–81.

Nyland, C. (1990). Capitalism and the history of work-time thought. In *The sociology of time* (pp. 130–151). Springer.

OECD. (2016). The labour market impacts of ill-health. In *Health at a glance: Europe 2016: State of health in the EU cycle*. OECD.

Pagán, R. (2013). Time allocation of disabled individuals. *Social Science and Medicine, 84*, 80–93.

Pan, A., Schernhammer, E. S., Sun, Q., & Hu, F. B. (2011). Rotating night shift work and risk of type 2 diabetes: Two prospective cohort studies in women. *PLoS Medicine, 8*(12), e1001141.

Park, C. Y., Lee, M. A., & Epstein, A. J. (2009). Variation in emergency department wait times for children by race/ethnicity and payment source. *Health Services Research, 44*(6), 2022–2039.

Pell, J. P., Hart, J. T., Pell, A. C., Norrie, J., Ford, I., & Cobbe, S. M. (2000). Effect of socioeconomic deprivation on waiting time for cardiac surgery: Retrospective cohort studyCommentary: Three decades of the inverse care law. *BMJ, 320*(7226), 15–19.

Presser, H. B. (2000). Nonstandard work schedules and marital instability. *Journal of Marriage and Family, 62*(1), 93–110.

Ray, K. N., Chari, A. V., Engberg, J., Bertolet, M., & Mehrotra, A. (2015). Disparities in time spent seeking medical care in the United States. *JAMA Internal Medicine, 175*(12), 1983–1986.

Roberts, J., Rice, N., & Jones, A. M. (2010). Early retirement among men in Britain and Germany: How important is health? *The Geneva Papers on Risk and Insurance – Issues and Practice, 35*(4), 644–667. https://doi.org/10.1057/gpp.2010.24

Rose, D. (2007). Food stamps, the Thrifty Food Plan, and meal preparation: The importance of the time dimension for US nutrition policy. *Journal of Nutrition Education and Behavior, 39*(4), 226–232.

Rydell, S. A., Harnack, L. J., Oakes, J. M., Story, M., Jeffery, R. W., & French, S. A. (2008). Why eat at fast-food restaurants: Reported reasons among frequent consumers. *Journal of the American Dietetic Association, 108*(12), 2066–2070.

Sargent, G. M., Banwell, C., Strazdins, L., & Dixon, J. (2018). Time and participation in workplace health promotion: Australian qualitative study. *Health Promotion International, 33*(3), 436–447.

Scambler, G. (2007). Social structure and the production, reproduction and durability of health inequalities. *Social Theory & Health, 5*(4), 297–315.

Semega, J. L., Fontenot, K. R., & Kollar, M. A. (2017). Income and poverty in the United States: 2016. *Current Population Reports* (P60-259).

Shove, E., Trentmann, F., & Wilk, R. R. (2009). *Time, consumption and everyday life: Practice, materiality and culture*. Berg.

Stansfeld, S. A., North, F., White, I., & Marmot, M. G. (1995). Work characteristics and psychiatric disorder in civil servants in London. *Journal of Epidemiology & Community Health, 49*(1), 48–53.

Strazdins, L., Clements, M. S., Korda, R. J., Broom, D. H., & D'Souza, R. M. (2006). Unsociable work? Nonstandard work schedules, family relationships, and children's well-being. *Journal of Marriage and Family, 68*(2), 394–410.

Strazdins, E., Dwan, K., Pescud, M., & Strazdins, L. (2019). Part-time in general practice—A remedy to a time-based problem? *Family Practice, 36*(4), 511–515.

Strazdins, L., Welsh, J., Korda, R., Broom, D., & Paolucci, F. (2016). Not all hours are equal: Could time be a social determinant of health? *Sociology of Health & Illness, 38*(1), 21–42.

Sugiyama, T., Salmon, J., Dunstan, D. W., Bauman, A. E., & Owen, N. (2007). Neighborhood walkability and TV viewing time among Australian adults. *American Journal of Preventive Medicine, 33*(6), 444–449.

Tada, Y., Kawano, Y., Maeda, I., Yoshizaki, T., Sunami, A., Yokoyama, Y., et al. (2014). Association of body mass index with lifestyle and rotating shift work in J apanese female nurses. *Obesity, 22*(12), 2489–2493.

Täht, K., & Mills, M. (2016). Nonstandard work schedules and partnership dissolution. In *Out of time* (pp. 91–112). Springer.

Tucker, R. C., Marx, K., & Engels, F. (1978). *The Marx-Engels reader.* Norton.

Van der Hulst, M. (2003). Long workhours and health. *Scandinavian Journal of Work, Environment & Health, 29*(3), 171–188.

Van Drongelen, A., Boot, C. R., Merkus, S. L., Smid, T., & Van Der Beek, A. J. (2011). The effects of shift work on body weight change—A systematic review of longitudinal studies. *Scandinavian Journal of Work, Environment & Health, 37*(4), 263–275.

Venn, D., & Strazdins, L. (2017). Your money or your time? How both types of scarcity matter to physical activity and healthy eating. *Social Science & Medicine, 172*, 98–106.

Volkoff, S., Buisset, C., & Mardon, C. (2010). Does intense time pressure at work make older employees more vulnerable? A statistical analysis based on a French survey "SVP50". *Applied Ergonomics, 41*(6), 754–762.

West, S. G., & Hepworth, J. T. (1991). Statistical issues in the study of temporal data: Daily experiences. *Journal of Personality, 59*(3), 609–662.

Zoer, I., Ruitenburg, M., Botje, D., Frings-Dresen, M., & Sluiter, J. (2011). The associations between psychosocial workload and mental health complaints in different age groups. *Ergonomics, 54*(10), 943–952.

3

Equity: How the Way We Use Time Creates Inequality

Abstract In almost all countries where it is measured women work more hours in the home while men work more hours to earn income. This simple disparity in time sets the scene for global gender inequality. Long work hours drive an either-or system which pits care against work, and it plays out in most households and societies. In some long-hour economies catastrophic fertility rates are a response, in others it is the persisting gender division in hours and earnings. Workplace tournaments mean that merit has become reframed as rewarding how long people work and how much they can do, rather than their quality and capability. Along with this gender hour-glass ceiling, generational overload adds another element. Young people now spend more time in education than ever before, and for them, the time tournament begins before they enter the labour market while they are building their skills and credentials.

Keywords Gender inequality • Hour-glass ceiling • Generational inequality • Time tournament • Work and family

© The Author(s), under exclusive license to Springer Nature Singapore Pte Ltd. 2024
L. Strazdins, *The Unequal Hour*, https://doi.org/10.1007/978-981-97-6337-5_3

A new word is entering the Japanese lexicon—*Wan ope ikuji*—it means 'one-person operation' (Sha, 2017). It describes the predicament of Japanese mothers, at home with their children, whose husbands don't come home during the week. It's a lonely word—a word about isolation and exclusion. It is better understood in the context of other Japanese words like 'karōshi' (death caused by overwork) and 'ganbaru' (the virtue of effort). What all these words mean is that long working hours are expected, well past government regulations of 40 hours per week. Nearly a third of the entire labour market works between 8 and 10 hours each day, and a fifth work even longer (Kobayashi et al., 2011). When we also consider long commute times, it makes sense why some Japanese workers don't go home. Among heterosexual couples most are men, and they bear a cost in terms of their sleep, their relationships, their opportunity to be with their babies and sometimes in the case of *karōshi*, their lives.

This lonely 'one-person operation' is not just playing out within families, it is playing out in the whole nation. It shows up in the dramatic plummet in fertility that's been going on for the last 40 years. Japanese fertility has stayed well below the numbers needed to stabilise population. It means fewer young people are being born to support the elderly. This is placing pressure on the government and the (dwindling) working age taxpayers to support the aged, but there is an even bigger economic disaster looming. Predictions indicate that by 2060, the Japanese population could shrink by nearly a third (National Institute of Population Social Security Research, 2012). This is a catastrophe on an unprecedented scale. This would mean a massive cut in the number of people who can work and pay taxes, consume and keep the economy going, have more babies or even care for many of the elderly. It can be traced back to the either-or system of long work hours versus care that pivots on time. It means if women want to earn a decent income in Japan they must stop having babies. And many have. It is costly no matter which way you look at it, and of course it is extraordinarily unequal.

This either-or work/care system is not just a problem in Japan (although Japan is an extreme example). It is found in labour markets where long work hours are viewed as normal (Messenger & Ray, 2013) and it was the norm in most Western countries until 1970. While progress has been made on the exclusion of women from paid work and men from caregiving in some countries, in others, women still face unsurmountable time hurdles to earning their way out of poverty. For example, a recent OECD (2015) report on gender inequality and development describes the day of a typical Ghanaian woman. In Ghana, like most developing countries, work hours are long and unregulated (ILO, 2007). In this example, her workday is very long—it averages 13 hours and has two parts. One part doesn't earn her any money and one part does. She cares for children, cooks, fetches water, collects firewood, washes, cleans and runs errands. All of this is essential, and takes 8 hours, but none of it earns money. She then adds on about 4 or 5 hours to try to sell goods, go to the market and do what she can to earn money. Meanwhile, her husband spends around 2½ hours of his day doing work that is not paid, and the rest of his time is spent earning money. In Ghana, most people need to work long hours to earn enough, since pay is low, so more than three quarters of Ghanaian wage workers spend between 41–50 hours working per week (Honorati & Johansson de Silva, 2016).

It is impossible to add these paid hours into a Ghanaian woman's day, so she will never earn money at the same rate as the men do. And, if she has no husband, or he loses his job, the essential but unpaid work does not go away, it must be done by someone. Typically, this work gets delegated to girls, who are taken out of school (a lifelong opportunity cost), and the gendered poverty trap lives on (Ferrant et al., 2014).

This is a root problem driving the feminisation of poverty that Melinda Gates named in her 2016 letter (Gates & Gates, 2016). She's got it—it's a time problem which creates an opportunity problem which creates a money problem which creates a gender equality problem, and all also create a health problem. For billions. And this interlinking of time, opportunity, money, health and gender is going on around the globe, in countries rich and poor.

3.1   Success: All Hours and No Care?

What does success look like when you consider earnings? Who are the top earners and what hours do they work to get there? Using data on employed Australians aged up to 65, we found that the vast majority (eight out of ten) of top earners are men and they work an average of 50 hours per week (Strazdins et al., paper under review). This is 12 hours per week longer than the national full-time standard of 38. As the earnings go down, so do the hours, and the percentages of women go up. There is a sweet spot—about 39 hours per week—where men and women are closely equal in their earnings and their hours, although neither are earning top dollar. As you look further down the income scale, hours continue to reduce. Eight out of ten of the lowest earners and shortest hour workers are women, a kind of labour market homoeostasis.

Sounds fair? It makes sense that if you work fewer hours, you earn less. So, the same goes for working longer hours, doesn't it? Is this still true if those hours are well beyond those meant to be worked in a full-time working week? This is the reward for effort, right? The question is, whose effort?

3.1.1 Gender Difference

As hours go up, so do the proportion of men (relative to women) who work them. This gender difference is no accident, nor is it about merit—it is because those long work hours are impossible to combine with running households or raising children. So, something and someone must give. To earn good money in Australia, as in many countries—to be senior, successful, influential *and* have a family—you need (along with other things) someone who is willing to free your time to do so. Behind those top earner statistics is a high price paid. Assuming a heterosexual household, one half of those high earning men have a female partner who redirects her time out of the labour force to help him succeed in it. But it's a different picture for a woman in these households—almost no woman gets this type of help with her time from a male partner, regardless of her occupation or seniority level. Therefore, this time gap drives an earnings gap and shows up in a seniority, wealth and power gap.

Deciding whether this is fair is trickier. Australian women have the same or better education, skills and capabilities compared to men. We want rewards to reflect merit, and we want gender equity, so why aren't women—who have equal skills—achieving equal rewards and income?

Many have suggested that women should just work longer hours to achieve equal rewards, while they keep doing nearly double the amount of unpaid work (OECD, 2020). We have only ever considered that the way to equality is for women to do more—because that seems to be all that is on offer. It's women's only option.

If that doesn't sound fair, then perhaps men should do more too. This would mean adding more of the unpaid work onto their long work hours, which we already know is impacting their health, so that everyone is equally overloaded. This is what is happening in our job market. In the past 20 years, we have witnessed a gradual (and modest) increase in men's time in family care, but no corresponding reduction in work hours (Craig & Mullan, 2012). Instead, a good job and a good income has remained conditional on working long full-time hours, so they have barely changed. Meanwhile, women have added on part-time paid work to domestic work and care. Everyone is doing more.

The reason we have imagined that gender equality can be achieved by doing more is that we have forgotten the simple, fixed and finite problem of time, and it has not worked. Women *have* entered the labour market, and they *are* doing more, and now the historical education and opportunity differentials have been reborn into pay gaps and time burdens. So now women (and many men), lead a no-rest, rushed, stressed and still unequal life. Only men or women who free themselves from care or domestic work, or any other non-work commitment on their time, succeed, but at the expense of those who don't. Does this still sound fair?

In a country like Australia, it means that for the same type of work and with the same qualification, a man earns AUD$100 but a woman earns AUD$79[1] (WGEA, 2020). It is virtually the same in the US, UK and Canada, where individuals make good incomes conditional on long hours. In some countries like Japan, Ghana ("Gender Gap Africa," 2020) and South Korea the difference ranges from $58 to $65 for every $100 a man earns, and it is no coincidence that in countries with huge pay gaps, the hours expected in a 'good' job are even longer. Over a lifetime, the

---

[1] This is the total remuneration gender pay gap rather than the base salary gender pay gap. In addition to base salary, this measure also accounts for additional benefits such as bonuses, performance pay, superannuation, overtime and other allowances.

difference in earnings becomes vast. Even in countries where women have the same legal rights, without equal time they are unlikely to ever achieve equal income. If they seek to work like men do, they are at risk of trading off their health, and that is not gender equality.

3.2   Time Tournaments

The fundamental problem is that time is viewed as central to success in the labour market, yet it is one of the most constrained resources people have (or don't have!). It is so important to our ideas of profitability and success that putting limits on how long people work and how available they should be seems counterintuitive. This framing of work hours as critical to success (one's own career or a business's profitability) has been reinforced by neoliberal ideas of free markets (Harvey, 2005). It's not that this hasn't been contested, but over the past 40 years there has been a weakening of legal limits on work hours (Harvey, 2005). At the low end, poverty and lower wages drive people to work long hours or be available for any shift or gig, if it is offered. People compete for jobs by being available, and they keep them with putting in extra effort, sometimes working well beyond the official hours.

It is easy to understand why people work long hours to try and work their way out of poverty. But why are hours so long in well-paid jobs, especially among men? This process is revealing because it shows how time has become so important to success that it drives behaviours even among the well paid, where success is defined as having a job or advancing in a job. According to organisational and management scholars Olivia O'Neill and Charles O'Reilly (2010), careers unfold as a series of tournaments where employees compete for advancement and rewards. Just as in actual tournaments, success is a combination of effort and ability; those with less ability or motivation do not progress, and this leaves similarly capable, motivated and talented people to compete. When everyone has equal merit, the competitive edge shifts to effort. And time—both availability and hours on the job—is seen as synonymous with effort. Lacking an upper limit on work hours or workloads, doing more becomes the de facto criteria for advancement. Hour for hour it may not be more productive (Lee & Lim, 2017), and in the long run there may be a health cost, but there is no doubt that a person who works 60 hours per week can produce more than someone who works 38. It is obvious what the incentive is.

3.2.1 Allowable Hours

Unfortunately, this pushes women out; countries with long weekly work hours show the widest employment inequality between men and women. It makes a surprising difference irrespective of a nation's affluence. Liana Christin Landivar (2015) compared 23 countries (all economically developed) in terms of the maximum weekly hours allowed under labour laws. She shows that as allowable hours went up, so did the gender gaps in work hours within households. She gives the example of Switzerland with a maximum work week of 64 hours. The gender gap in work time within a Swiss couple was 6.3 hours per week more than in a Finnish couple. In Finland, the maximum weekly work hours are 45 and better enforced. The lower the maximum hour standard—and the more strictly enforced— the narrower the nation's gender gap in work hours and labour force participation.

This long-hour problem is worsening, not improving. In countries like the US, long-hour workers (50 hours or more a week) are experiencing the greatest wage growth, which means time is delivering even more rewards, and it is becoming the edge on which workers compete. In 1979, people who worked more than 50 hours each week did not get paid more per hour for doing so. About one in eight US workers worked long hours, but this did not deliver them, hour for hour, higher wages (in fact if pay was averaged over the extra hours, it was lower). But by 1999, working 50 hours or more led to an increase in wage returns *per hour*—of 4% (for men) and 2% (for women). By 2009 the wage premium (think of this as a bonus or reward for working long hours) was 6% for both men and women. But few women worked them, so the hours started to matter more to the gender gaps in earning than skills, job experience or education (Cha & Weeden, 2014). When faced with a rising work-hour bar, women's options are to do even more, or cut back their hours or leave the workforce altogether when they have any other demands on their time (Maume, 2006). These options pit health against equality.

3.2.2 Australia's Version

Australia doesn't show the same extreme pattern as Japan or the US. We have more options for short-hour jobs, and so this forces families into an extreme either-or system of who works for money and who works for the family. Instead of not working at all, the Australian version of *wan ope ikuji* (one person operation) is that women work short hours or part time. Australia does not have the same low fertility crisis either, but it still has a gender wage gap, tied to this gender hour gap, that doesn't budge. Right now, at least one quarter of all employed Australians work past the National Employment Standard of 38 weekly work hours. One in 10 Australians work 41–49 hours per week, more than one in eight work longer than 50 hours. And it is getting worse, not better, even while gender equality is being promoted. For example, in July 2010, on average, full-time Australian men worked 41.0 weekly hours compared with 35.8 hours for full-time women—a difference of about 4.1 hours more than full-time women. This calculates out to 16.4 additional hours per month, or 180.4 hours per year, assuming 1-month leave. This creates a clear advantage in the 'job tournament' to secure the high paying, better earning jobs and it is rising not falling. Thirty years ago in Australia, full-time men worked an average of just 1.4 hours more than full-time women (ABS, 2010).

3.3   The Hour-Glass Ceiling

This brings me to the health part of the problem. Working 50 hours or more per week, by anyone's standard, man or woman, is likely to be hazardous to health. The International Labour Organisation defines 48 hours as the safe limit up to which people should work (ILO, 2011). However, this definition is outdated because it was set when the labour market was almost entirely male. He might have been able to work 48 hours, but this was because he didn't need to come home and cook, clean and care for children, run errands or manage the household. Women do this, and we have not yet defined a safe work-hour standard that includes them.

I have had the great pleasure of working with talented econometricians and epidemiologists, Huong Dinh and Jenny Welsh. We worked together to estimate the health costs of the real work week. What I mean by real is that we considered the way both paid and unpaid hours affect health, and then explored the way, this time, earnings and health trade-off locked in gender inequality in the labour market (Dinh et al., 2017). One of the advances in the study was modelling the earnings, time and health system using statistical estimates that could calculate the back and forth relationships between people's health, what they could earn and what hours they worked, on and off the job. All of this was estimated in the context of how much time they did or didn't spend in care and domestic work. This meant we didn't model time and health as a simple one-way type of problem, we allowed for all the different pathways that knit time, money, gender and health together—the keystone idea raised in Chap. 2. The study used a large representative sample of employed Australians: men, women, young, middle-aged and old. The first thing we did was look at how work hours affected mental health, and what we found was a tipping point. Averaging over every person in the labour market we found that working at least some hours was good for people. Mental health improved, probably because jobs deliver a sense of identity, security, status, friendships and the feeling of inclusion. The more hours people worked the better their score, but only up to a point. And that point was 39 hours per week. After that, mental health started to deteriorate. Think of it as an inverted U. We thought of it as a health ceiling, and the gender gap in this ceiling we called the *hour-glass ceiling*.

3.3.1 Health Tipping Points

Because the 39 hours averages over everything and everybody, it doesn't consider differences in jobs, income, or having a partner who is at home (as heterosexual men usually have)—differences that are also linked to gender. So, we cut the sample into two, and estimated the work-hour tipping point separately for employed men and employed women. The story changed. That original average of 39 hours per week hid a large gender difference. For women, the tipping point was 34 hours per week, after which their mental health declined. But for men, they could work up to 47 hours per week before they showed any detriment to their mental health. This is a 13-hour difference in weekly work hours. It means an Australian man can, every week, average 13 hours longer on his job than a woman can before he starts to trade-off his mental health. This delivers a huge time advantage in the job tournament, and it is a pretty good explanation for why gender pay gaps haven't changed and why we have so few women in senior roles. These health harms further disadvantage women, and are especially likely in the higher earning and senior jobs, where long hours are expected and women are underrepresented. We saw the hour-glass ceiling as another, hidden part of the glass ceiling.

But why was the tipping point that much higher for men? This is a question we wanted to answer. So, we divided the sample another way, by how much time was spent in (unpaid) care and domestic work. We did this roughly, simply dividing people into the top and bottom 50%. Then we recalculated tipping points. And we saw a very similar pattern to the ones we calculated by gender. Anyone who spends more time than the average employed Australian on unpaid work showed a similar tipping point to the one we found for women—34 hours. Of course, if a person has no caring demands or does very little domestic work, then they can work long hours before affecting their health (the tipping points for both men and women are close to the ILO's 48 hours). This is the work-hour limit that might have made sense when the workforce was almost entirely men (but rested on the invisible and unpaid workforce that was almost entirely women). This is the problem of Japan, or of any country where long hours are expected and rewarded, and the time tournament at work is encouraged or unrestrained. People can only manage long hours (and minimise the trade-off on their health) if they don't care or do domestic work. Or else they must sacrifice time for exercising, eating healthy food or adequate sleep. Something must give, since there are only 24 hours in a day. Working long hours is what gets rewarded—but it's completely unsustainable if we want gender equity.

If men pick up more care and domestic work, their tipping point starts to approximate women's. This means they compromise their health sooner than male counterparts who do not. The time health trade-off locks women out of the labour market. If they seek to be equal and work like men, they will compromise their health. The time health trade-off locks men out of sharing care. If they seek to be the fathers many of them long to be, they are unlikely to hold onto their good jobs and they will compromise their health. Like women, they begin to suffer a competitive disadvantage in the workplace if work hours are effectively unlimited, nothing based on merit but all based on time. This is the keystone I was talking about in Chap. 2. It locks gender inequality into the labour market and generates health trade-offs. It locks gendered income inequality and the feminisation of poverty into society. It excludes women who have a family from the political process and power because their voices are not heard on corporate boards, in leadership roles or in politics unless they are among the very few whose husband reverses his role. It is work *or* care, men *or* women, never both. Health plays a part, because it will become compromised if people try to exceed their time limit. It's the first thing they cut back. This is the inequitable pressures on people's time that public health hasn't grappled with. And it needs to.

Of course, not all households comprise a husband and wife. In same-sex households, assumptions of gender don't seem to drive time divisions of earnings and care. Time, earnings and tasks are more evenly shared in these families, raising questions about the role power and time play to lock in the work—care dichotomy. Bauer (2016) studied gender roles and the division of domestic work and earnings in same-sex and different-sex households in Austria, Belgium, France, the Netherlands, Norway, Sweden and Australia. Same-sex couples earned more equally and overall earned more than their heterosexual counterparts. Martell and Roncolato (2020) compared time spent on household tasks by women in same- and different-sex households, finding that while heterosexual women exhibited a U-shape relationship between earnings share and household labour, lesbians exhibited the inverse. This separation between gender, earnings and care is evident for both male and female same-sex couples, although male same-sex couples collectively spend more time in paid employment than female same-sex couples (Grossbard & Jepsen, 2008; van der Vleuten et al., 2021).

3.4   Generational Overload: The Future of Work (and Study)

Type the words 'future of work' into any search engine and you will get millions of hits. Reports, government enquiries, analyses, scenarios, news articles, blogs and commentaries. Some raise the spectre of mass unemployment and job loss. Others reassure that, just as we always have, we will re-adjust and new jobs will emerge. Some place our work futures in the context of other demographic, social, environmental and economic changes that are looming, like the ageing population with lifespans that are 30 or 40 years longer than ever before (bringing with them the need for extended working lives), or the massive surge in global population (and global mobility) bringing with it greater pressures on resources and greater competition for jobs. All of these changes are taking place in the reworking of a new world order where the economic might is shifting to Asia. Now, relatively privileged and regulated labour markets are competing cheek by economic jowl with countries with lower wages, little regulation and very long work hours. Then there is climate change and species loss, placing further pressures on water, land, food and energy (more uncharted territory), not to mention the evolving transformation in how societies connect, produce, do business and communicate as we go fully digital and artificial intelligence technology expands. So much has been written about how this future will pan out in terms of people's jobs and their livelihoods. But few ask the question of how this future will shape people's time and their health. Will we need to do more or do less to earn money and secure a job? Will technology and AI relieve us of time? How might the time tournament evolve if competition for jobs ramps up?

Actually the future of work is already happening (Hajkowicz et al., 2016). There's a generation growing up, right now, for whom this constantly changing, digitised and ultra-competitive 'future' *is* their world. They are living the changes, they are the frontline and are finding that the labour market they are entering has raised the bar on both effort and credentials. Education has become more expensive *and* more essential. Meanwhile, there is no guarantee that once this education is completed there will be a good job. In fact, under accelerating pressures of rapid change in jobs and services, education may never be completed. Yes, they are technologically savvy, yes, they are always connected, yes, they are familiar with rapid change and rapid obsolescence. Except, now this rapid change and obsolescence is not just about gadgets, devices or new technologies, it's also about jobs, skills and livelihoods. This cohort of young adults, and the ones following them, are facing more income uncertainty and more labour market competition, which makes the job tournament even tougher—and it has started earlier. To add to this, they also now face requirements to continually learn and change. They must hold down jobs *and* keep learning to stay in the race. This is creating inequality, through time, that reaches across generations. For the younger generation, pressure isn't stemming as much from work and family (although this is looming as an added predicament), it's about work and study, and this section explores this through the lens of time.

3.4.1 Education Tournament

For this generation, the time tournament begins *before* they enter the labour market, while they are building their skills and credentials. It has resulted in young people spending more time in education or training than previous generations, spending more money to do so, and if their family cannot pay upfront, going into greater debt (Houle, 2014). In Australia, for example, to gain their skills, young people today are paying double what previous generations paid. They pay, on average, $26,000 for a 3-year undergraduate degree, in 1991 it was $10,000 and in 1985 it cost nothing (Statista, 2020). If they don't come from families who can financially support them, many take on a job, working so that they can afford to learn (Masevičiūte et al., 2018).

But, the yield from these major time and money investments is increasingly uncertain. For decades, a tertiary education has been the pathway to a good job, a way out of poverty and a way up socially. It has been a guarantee of good earnings, and a foot in the door for success. But that is changing for this generation. The UK think tank—Centre for Global Higher Education—sees another scenario opening up: underemployment (Green & Henseke, 2017). By underemployment they mean unable to find a job, or working in a job that neither requires nor rewards educational investment. Of course, some young adults will be able to start careers after finishing their study, but it is no longer a guarantee. The Centre for Global Higher Education predicts that rising numbers of graduates will struggle to find the job they were training for—prestigious, interesting and well-paid. Instead, they will find and work in 'lowly jobs'. This is not a problem of merit, or attitude, or quality, or training, it is simply a problem of scale. There are so many graduates, well-credentialed and ready, that good education is no longer sufficient. It is predicted that by 2030, China and India are expected to provide nearly 60% of the STEM qualified workforce for G20 countries (and half of all tertiary educated young people on the planet, OECD, 2015). Previous decades saw manufacturing jobs shift globally to countries with lower wages and standards of living. This global competition has now turned to technical and professional jobs, which require years of educational investment.

What happens when the need to obtain credentials increases, as does the number of people who have them, while the opportunities to reap their benefit reduces? This is a classic tournament. It means the pool of people with equal merit and skills who want to enter the labour market increases, so now the rewards shift to other metrics, like time, experience and (unpaid) training in the hoped-for profession. Once in a job it could sharpen the gender-hour gap, by putting upward pressure on hours worked. But the tournament extends to getting a job, not just advancing up the ranks. This pushes up demand for credentials, an undergraduate degree is not sufficient, so the success edge has shifted upwards. The result is studying for longer before getting a job, and then facing stiff competition to get and hold one. This is all expensive, very expensive, not just in terms of money, but also in terms of time, and this brings health trade-offs. In countries such as the US, Canada, Australia and the Netherlands, learner earners (adults who both work and study) are the majority (Quintini, 2015). This is not 1 or 2 hours a week or even 5 or 10, the average work hours among tertiary students in Europe are 28 per week (Masevičiūte et al., 2018) and full-time study is generally around 40. This is generational overload.

Few studies have considered how this ramping up of time and money costs plays out for people's health, even while it is clear many are in trouble. One exception is a study conducted by scholars Tessa Grimmond and Amelia Yazidjoglou. They were both studying while also working throughout their degree, living under pressure and seeing this in their peers. So, they studied it, interviewing more than 20 undergraduate students on the campus about their jobs, their degree, their hopes and their health. The young people they talked with convincingly articulated the dilemma. They described a life of choosing between lesser evils to earn their living while striving to get good grades, protecting their study one minute and compromising it the next. As one undergrad explained, "If you don't have financial stability it creates insane anxiety and stress right? So like, what's worse? The fear of not being able to pay your bills and getting credit-card debt? Or getting a C average? What causes more stress?" (Grimmond et al., 2020)

3.4.2 Impacts on Mental Health

These students weren't just feeling 'stressed', a majority were suffering from anxiety and depression at levels which constituted a mental-health condition. It was so endemic that many did not view symptoms such as broken sleep, worry and tension, sadness, difficulty relaxing or emotional lability as a problem. Instead, they were seen as part of being a student, and the health consequences a normal outcome. Breakdowns, exhaustion and episodes of extreme distress were, in the words of one young woman, "something to be expected" (Grimmond et al., 2020). Their time became a *jumbled mess*, never sure when it was for work or for study and which one mattered the most (Yazidjoglou, 2018). And not surprisingly—under this sort of pressure—time for health comes last. "I didn't have much time in the week that was down time it was all um either uni or work. I didn't have any time to just sort of sleep or de-stress or anything" (Full-time employed, studying part time, Yazidjoglou, 2018). It is understandable, but it brings with it a potentially long-lasting health cost.

Researchers are documenting rising rates of chronic illness, mental and physical, among this age group, which are potentially increasing disease burdens over the life course and compromising life spans (Ho & Hendi, 2018). US figures reveal major depressive episodes are increasing among young adults and adolescents by more than 50% (Twenge et al., 2019). In the UK, almost one in five young people report depression or anxiety, a 5% increase to rates 10 years previously (Thorley, 2017). One in eight Australians aged 18 to 24 reports extreme mental distress, a 5% jump from rates 6 years earlier (ARACY, 2018).

3.4.3 Impacts on Physical Health

Not only is this generation at greater risk with their mental health, but they are also getting heavier, which means they will be more prone to metabolic, cardiovascular and other chronic diseases. Almost one half of young Australians are overweight or obese, up from 40% in 2014 and 2015 (ABS, 2019), trends that mirror those of the US (CDC, 2020) and UK (Baker, 2019). Diabetes type II is going up (Charles et al., 2015), and the time-dependent behaviours that would avert it, such as physical activity, are going down. The US surgeon general warns that nearly half of American youths aged 12–21 are not meeting physical activity minima (CDC, 1999). The same inactivity is concerningly observed among young Australians (AIHW, 2019) while less than 4% eat sufficient fresh fruit and vegetables daily (ABS, 2019). These trends do not necessarily turn around as these young adults age (more than half of young Americans aged 25–30 eat on the run, and are too rushed to eat a healthy breakfast, Escoto et al., 2012).

This decline in health-protective behaviours is likely to set at least some onto a downward health trajectory, creating vulnerabilities in capability that shape jobs and relational futures as well as lifespans. This generation is caught between pressures to succeed by increasing their education, and the need to work to do so. It is a ratcheting up of pressure, particularly on their time, with the potential to generate health inequities that add generation to race, gender and class.

In this chapter I've tried to explain how time is an essential dimension of inequality, both gender and generational, but it's gone under the radar, and its a drag on our health (Fig. 3.1) I've also hoped to explain that there is a current and a future problem for a more equal and healthy society, and we need a social conversation about it. Are job tournaments fair?

Fig. 3.1 Erin I Walsh Time drag 2024

Should we reward people on their time more than on their quality? Should we limit long work hours or let individuals and families work it out? How will AI change pressures to work longer or be constantly available, will the pressure go up or down? How do we help the future generations with the costly need to keep studying, usually while they keep working? And there's the need to see the link to our health. Government needs to see this link. The health care system needs to see this link. Public health campaigners need to see this link. The next chapter is about action and possibilities that could be considered, especially those that might help protect our health.

References

ABS. (2010). *6105.0 – Australian labour market statistics, October*. Australian Bureau of Statistics.

ABS. (2019). *National health survey: First results, 2017–18. 4364.0.55.001.* Australian Bureau of Statistics.

AIHW. (2019). *Insufficient physical activity. PHE 248.* Australian Institute of Health and Welfare.

ARACY. (2018). *Report card 2018: The wellbeing of young Australians.* Australian Research Alliance for Children and Youth.

Baker, C. (2019). *Briefing paper: 3336 – Obesity statistics.* The House of Commons Library.

Bauer, G. (2016). Gender roles, comparative advantages and the life course: The division of domestic labor in same-sex and different-sex couples. *European Journal of Population / Revue Européenne de Démographie, 32*(1), 99–128.

CDC. (1999). *A report of the surgeon general- physical activity and health: Adolescents and young adults.* Centers for Disease Control and Prevention.

CDC. (2020). *Overweight and obesity: Adult obesity facts.* Centers for Disease Control and Prevention. https://www.cdc.gov/obesity/data/adult.html

Cha, Y., & Weeden, K. A. (2014). Overwork and the slow convergence in the gender gap in wages. *American Sociological Review, 79*(3), 457–484. https://doi.org/10.1177/0003122414528932

Charles, J., Pollack, A., & Britt, H. (2015). Type 2 diabetes and obesity in young adults. *Australian Family Physician, 44,* 269–270.

Craig, L., & Mullan, K. (2012). Australian fathers' work and family time in comparative and temporal perspective. *Journal of Family Studies, 18*(2–3), 165–174.

Dinh, H., Strazdins, L., & Welsh, J. (2017). Hour-glass ceilings: Work-hour thresholds, gendered health inequities. *Social Science & Medicine, 176,* 42–51.

Escoto, K. H., Laska, M. N., Larson, N., Neumark-Sztainer, D., & Hannan, P. J. (2012). Work hours and perceived time barriers to healthful eating among young adults. *American Journal of Health Behavior, 36*(6), 786–796.

Ferrant, G., Pesando, L. M., & Nowacka, K. (2014). *Unpaid care work: The missing link in the analysis of gender gaps in labour outcomes.* OECD Development Center.

Gates, B., & Gates, M. (2016). *Two superpowers we wish we had: Melinda and I want more time and energy—For everyone.* https://www.gatesnotes.com/2016-Annual-Letter

Gender Gap Africa. (2020). https://gendergap.africa/

Green, F., & Henseke, G. (2017). *Graduates and 'graduate jobs' in Europe: A picture of growth and diversification* (p. 47). Centre for Global Higher Education. Working paper series, 25.

Grimmond, T., Yazidjoglou, A., & Strazdins, L. (2020). Earning to learn: The time-health trade-offs of employed Australian undergraduate students. *Health Promotion International, 35*(6), 1302–1311. https://doi.org/10.1093/heapro/daz133

Grossbard, S., & Jepsen, L. K. (2008). The economics of gay and lesbian couples: Introduction to a special issue on gay and lesbian households. *Review of Economics of the Household, 6*(4), 311–325.

Hajkowicz, S., Reeson, A., Rudd, L., Bratanova, A., Hodgers, L., Mason, C., & Boughen, N. (2016). *Tomorrow's Digitally Enabled Workforce: Megatrends and scenarios for jobs and employment in Australia over the coming twenty years.* CSIRO.

Harvey, D. (2005). *A brief history of neoliberalism.* Oxford University Press.

Ho, J. Y., & Hendi, A. S. (2018). Recent trends in life expectancy across high income countries: Retrospective observational study. *BMJ (Clinical Research Ed.), 362*, k2562–k2562. https://doi.org/10.1136/bmj.k2562

Honorati, M., & Johansson de Silva, S. (2016). *Expanding job opportunities in Ghana.* The World Bank.

Houle, J. N. (2014). A generation indebted: Young adult debt across three cohorts. *Social Problems, 61*(3), 448–465.

ILO. (2007). *Trends in working time.* International Labour Organization.

ILO. (2011). *Working time in the twenty-first century.* International Labour Organization.

Kobayashi, T., Morofuji, E., & Watanabe, Y. (2011). *Sleeping time keeps decreasing, male housework time is increasing. From the 2010 NHK Japanese Time Use Survey.* https://www.nhk.or.jp/bunken/english/reports/summary/201104/01.html

Landivar, L. C. (2015). The gender gap in employment hours: Do work hour regulations matter? *Work, Employment and Society, 29*(4), 550–570.

Lee, D., & Lim, H. (2017). Multiple thresholds in the nexus between working hours and productivity. *Contemporary Economic Policy, 35*(4), 716–734.

Martell, M. E., & Roncolato, L. (2020). Share of household earnings and time use of women in same-sex and different-sex households. *Eastern Economic Journal, 46*(3), 414–437. https://www.jstor.org/stable/48730460

Masevičiūtė, K., Šaukeckienė, V., & Ozolinčiūtė, E. (2018). *Combining studies and paid jobs: Thematic review.* EUROSTUDENT.

Maume, D. J. (2006). Gender differences in restricting work efforts because of family responsibilities. *Journal of Marriage and Family, 68*, 859–869.

Messenger, J. C., & Ray, N. (2013). *The distribution of hours of work in developed and developing countries: What are the main differences and why?* International Labour Organization.

National Institute of Population Social Security Research. (2012). *Population projections for Japan (January 2012): 2011 to 2060.* National Institute of Population and Social Security Research.

O'Neill, O. A., & O'Reilly, C. (2010). Careers as tournaments: The impact of sex and gendered organizational culture preferences in MBA's income attainment. *Journal of Organizational Behaviour, 31*, 856–876.

OECD. (2015). *Education indicators in focus: How is the global talent pool changing?* OECD.

OECD. (2020). *Employment: Time spent in paid and unpaid work, by sex.* https://stats.oecd.org/index.aspx?queryid=54757

Quintini, G. (2015). *Working and learning: A diversity of patterns.* OECD.

Sha, J. K. (2017). *The words of 2017.* https://www.nippon.com/en/features/c03806/

Statista. (2020). *Average cost of a three-year undergraduate degree in Australia from 1985 to 2016.* https://www.statista.com/statistics/693291/australia-average-cost-undergraduate-degree/

Thorley, C. (2017). *Not by degrees: Improving student mental health in the UK's universities.* IPPR.

Twenge, J. M., Cooper, A. B., Joiner, T. E., Duffy, M. E., & Binau, S. G. (2019). Age, period, and cohort trends in mood disorder indicators and suicide-related outcomes in a nationally representative dataset, 2005–2017. *Journal of Abnormal Psychology, 128*(3), 185–199.

van der Vleuten, M., Jaspers, E., & van der Lippe, T. (2021). Same-sex couples' division of labor from a cross-national perspective. *Journal of GLBT Family Studies, 17*(2), 150–167. https://doi.org/10.1080/1550428X.2020.1862012

WGEA. (2020). *The gender pay gap.* https://www.wgea.gov.au/topics/the-gender-pay-gap

Yazidjoglou, A. (2018). *Consequences of combining work and study: Time and health trade-offs.* Masters of Public Health thesis, Australian National University.

4

Action: Time to Change?

Abstract There is no pill for more time. No vaccine or doctor that can cure it and no shop to buy it, yet everyone needs time to be healthy, so what can be done about it? This chapter re-imagines change and gives examples. There are choices, but they are not just for individuals—workplaces, governments and communities could start by using design principles that enable more time for health. Governments, for example, could give back time to citizens by the way cities and transport are designed and technology used. Neighbourhoods could be planned to create win-wins for health, physical activity and community connection. And what would it be like if we simply had less paperwork? The chapter concludes with some successful experiments in giving more time on and off the job, all of which have benefitted health.

Keywords Human rights • Parental leave • Policymaking • Reduced work hours • Smart cities

There is no pill for more time. No vaccine or doctor that can cure it and no shop to buy it, yet everyone needs time to be healthy. If we believe what people tell us, then a lack of time is becoming a threat for a wide

© The Author(s), under exclusive license to Springer Nature Singapore Pte Ltd. 2024   **81**
L. Strazdins, *The Unequal Hour*, https://doi.org/10.1007/978-981-97-6337-5_4

range of diseases and malaises. So, what can be done about it? This chapter is about action. But before I start, let me say what this chapter is not about. It is not about time management. It is not about top tips to save time. You will not find a three-step programme, or a quick list of five things you must do to make time for your health.

What I want this book to do is help the reader understand why time is shaping health and for whom, as well as gain some ideas about what needs to change. I don't give (and don't have) answers, instead this chapter gives some short examples of where governments, town planners and health services have valued peoples' time and helped protect it. In my view, to have enough time to be healthy will only occur when everyone's time and everyone's health are taken seriously and valued.

Oliver Burkeman (2021) values time differently. He talks about the 4000 weeks of the average lifespan, and this countdown of weeks centres time as finite each day *and* each life. Lifespans are counted in weeks, and every week that passes is one less. And at some point, there are no more weeks. This creates urgency to focus on doing what matters, it re-values time (as finite and therefore precious) *and* elevates health, because we need both to live. This shifts 'time management' away from doing more for less to asking what we use our time for, knowing one day we will no longer have it. It is a mind-shift that applies to everyone, including institutions. Imagine if workplaces no longer saw their employee's time as an expandable and expendable resource to do more and keep coping? If administrators paused before they invented another bureaucratic process for people to do, and instead asked how much time this takes and how they will compensate for it? Or if town planners built transport systems and neighbourhoods to maximise healthy wins such as walking to work or school? And what would it mean for how health systems are designed, and how practitioners and health policy makers respond to community health needs if they did not assume unwell people and their caregivers can keep waiting?

There are lots of choices here, for individuals certainly, but also for workplaces, governments, town planners and health policymakers. The very first step is to value time and health—ours and others —more. Step two is to advocate, argue and get on with redesigning systems, cities, jobs, health interventions and health care systems in ways that prioritise time, respond to its 'finitude' and question the assumptions that the time of employees, citizens or health care consumers is 'free'. The ideas, evidence and examples from this last chapter may, I hope, support you in doing this.

4.1 Key Messages

The starting point for this pivot was that time is poetical, practical, deeply political *and* it is a resource we need for our health. This complexity matters, not just in understanding how important time is for health (revaluing), but for understanding what actions are needed and why they can be difficult to take. Below is a collection of some of the key ideas.

Time is practical and elusive. Time is like money in one way—it's a thing we need and use for just about all aspects of daily life that enable good health. But, unlike money, food, water or shelter, we can't see or touch it, it is not a tangible thing. That is the poetry of time—it can be deep, elusive and personal but this also means it is easily overlooked even while our daily lives are controlled by it. The author Peter S Beagle (2022, pp. 233–234) captured this concrete elusiveness when he wrote "I believed – as you do – that time was at least as real and solid as myself......I lived in a house bricked up with seconds and minutes, weekends and New Year's days, and I never went outside."

Time is political. Time is also, as I hope I have shown, a politically charged resource. We use our time to earn income, others pay us for our time and everyone wants the best deal. This means there are competing motivations and vested interests in how time is valued and struggles over any attempts to change this. Almost always, if I am talking or presenting on the need to re-value time for health, the very first problem raised is that any change to free up time for health, such as shorten work hours or improve how services are designed, will cost money. This is likely right, meanwhile it's costing health.

The value given to paid time outweighs the value given to unpaid time. I have been part of a team interviewing policy and business leaders about long work hours. We are finding that while many agree that long hours are harmful, they also think the hours their employees work is something that can't be changed or else the business would fail (they have no choice).

The choice shifts to employees to change their unpaid time (it's a personal choice to have other responsibilities such as caregiving, rather than being a workplace problem). While the need for and value of long work hours seems solid, clear and irrefutable, personal time is viewed as fluid and malleable, less important or else simply a matter of priorities.

What time means, and how time feels, has evolved. The experience of time was not always so closely tied to hours or minutes and efficiency (doing more in less time), and it is not the same in all countries or cultures. Technology and industrialisation sets most societies on a course of doing almost everything faster and this is recurring in the age of AI. This speed is unprecedented historically or culturally, it creates a feeling of rushing and pressure and this speeding up of the pace of life and rate of change is called social acceleration.

Paradoxically, technology and the pursuit of efficiency have put more pressures on time. Even while technologies have cut the time it takes to do almost everything, they have raised the expectation (and need) to do more. As a result, a new malaise has surfaced—the problem of work-life balance. What this means is that many people find that they lack time to 'live' despite striving for greater efficiency and using more technology. Difficult choices about time are a constant feature of most people's lives, and even as people do one thing, they feel guilty and worry that they should be doing another—so time has become a source of anxiety. Asking people, then, to allocate more time to health (it takes nearly an hour and a half to complete 10000 steps a day, walking moderately fast, and this is what is recommended to keep healthy) is asking many to do what is almost impossible. Rather than assume that if people say they lack time they are being lazy, crazy, unmotivated or mistaken, being healthy is competing for time in a scarce market.

Not all time can be used for health. Another key concept is the notion of usable time. There is a misconception that there is plenty of time for health, it is just that people make poor choices or are lazy. This drives the commonly voiced view that instead of watching TV everyone should just get off their couches. But usability depends on lots of factors. Such as the control people have over their time. For example, is any free time available in a decent chunk, or in fragments over the day? Can it be interrupted and easily disrupted? Can it be used, safely (an hour at midnight vs midday are completely different prospects for exercising)? What about 'free time' that involves responsibilities to others, such as being on call for the workplace or having to be in the same space as children or others, to care for them?

Excessive demands on time can be a health hazard. How time shapes health operates through multiple pathways, and one is as a *health hazard.* This is well documented when it comes to work time. Long work hours, nightshifts and unpredictable work times, inability to control time (inflexibility) and intensification (the pace of work) all can erode well-being, especially if they add onto other time demands such as care. The World Health Organization recently declared long work hours as one of the most serious global occupational health risks, estimating 488 million people are working longer than 55 hours a week (Pega et al., 2021).

Lack of time creates a barrier to healthy behaviours. When resources become scarce, any additional 'spend' is perceived to have a greater relative cost than if it was plentiful. Thus, for anyone who is busy, the cost of 'spending' time on health is even higher. In this way lack of time becomes a *barrier* to being healthy for many people during some of the most important decades of their lives, when they are working or raising families.

The less powerful wait longer. Time can also be used to punish, discriminate and disempower people in ways that affect health, through a process of *social weathering.* This is the idea that small, everyday social insults and inconveniences wear down bodies as well as minds. Thus, the less powerful wait longer for things they need (health care is one example), and the less powerful also work harder to earn money (the persistent gender wage gap means it costs women more time to earn the same money as a man).

Poor health limits how people use their time (especially for earning income), creating a downward spiral. Poor health restricts how people use their time, leading to *exclusion* (this is a reverse path). For example, mental illness, disability and many health conditions limit opportunities to gain and keep jobs. In a society that places a premium on efficiency, and where people are recruited and promoted because they can work long and fast, it's easy to see how poor health locks people out because of their limited time.

Time is a hallmark of inequality. Finally, the book discussed time as a core feature—a *keystone*—of social inequality. This is a bit counterintuitive because money is usually seen in this role. I have argued time is equally important at least in the market economies most of us live in. People use time to earn money, and this money can be used, to some extent, to buy things we need for health. But no one can endlessly use their time to earn without compromising health, so how this three-way trade-off is resolved is linked to power and privilege. Executives, for example, can earn far more for their time than a cleaner can, meanwhile the time needed to love, nurture and raise children or care for the sick or elderly is almost never paid at all. But it still must be done, for cleaner's and executive's children alike. This straightaway makes for tensions between how much (and whose) time can be used to earn money while having time available for health and for other valued roles. This drives inequality, especially gender inequality, because time is fundamental to opportunity, money, health and power.

Policies and interventions that don't consider time can harm health. The US Thrifty Food Plan described in Chap. 2 is a good example. It was a programme that was well-intentioned, but time blind. It meant poor American families, who were struggling with problems of income, exclusion and poor health, were asked to be healthy in ways that they could not possibly achieve. They could not spend the extra 16 hours each week, because it was time that they did not have—and so the plan did not improve their health. It resulted in quite the opposite. It simply added further time burdens to all their other hardships, increasing vulnerability and disenfranchisement (Davis & You, 2011). And, of course, this problem of time blindness was particularly, inequitably, affecting those who were least able to control their time: single parents, working-poor, women—digging them deeper into hardship. But it doesn't need to be that way. Here is a counter example.

Policies and interventions that value time can create win-wins for health and equity. Another US programme—Raising Successful Children— took a completely different approach. The aim was to support the parenting skills of high-risk families. The dropout rates for these types of programmes are usually between half to three quarters of families, often termed 'the hard to reach'. But this health intervention thought differently. The designers understood that lack of time, as well as lack of money and parenting support, was what they were up against—not lack of willingness. So, they addressed the time costs as well as the money costs of being in their programme. They scheduled sessions at times that suited parents. They supported them with transport to reduce travelling time because most did not have a car. They provided childcare on site. They gave children meals so when parents went home after the evening sessions, their children were fed and ready for bed. The result—nearly seven out of ten families stayed in their programme, an order of magnitude better than most (Dumka et al., 1997). Why? Because they made it feasible. They made it easy. And they valued time, both paid and unpaid. By doing so, they made good health and well-being accessible and equitable. They likely changed lives of whole families and they have shown how actions can be taken to free up time for health, which is the focus of the rest of this chapter.

4.2   Design Principles to Support Time for Health

The evidence is in, we know an hour a day keeps the doctor away, but how do we make sure people have it? Laura Ford and I found examples of policies and health-related interventions that addressed the problem of time, and we wrote a report about this for our local government, 'Cities for Our Time' (Strazdins & Ford, 2019). This section describes the design principles used by workplaces, city planners and health service providers to design interventions to free up time for health. I then give some selected examples of what they did.

There were four design principles that emerged from our review:

Some interventions focussed directly on *reducing* the time costs associated with them, for example, making services quicker, easier, simpler, shorter or making healthy food easy to purchase and prepare. Others *offset* the time costs of an activity to lessen pressures and time conflicts with other priorities. For example, one exercise campaign realised that they were not changing behaviour, so they added bylines in a new campaign encouraging people to combine exercise with other valued activities (such as walking and talking with their partner or children). No surprise, behaviour change increased (Strazdins et al., 2012). Third, *timing* helped make good health more 'affordable' by changing when services were open or where they were, so they were accessible, quicker, easier to get to and more convenient. After-hours health care, apps that help people park near destinations or know when services are on time, making neighbourhoods more walkable by locating houses close to services are all examples. Finally, policies and interventions that focused on a *better quality* of time, such as making exercise fun or safer, seemed to be successful. What connects all these principles is seriously considering time into the design and roll out of the policy.

Sean Innis, who spent decades leading national policy teams, delineated a process that governments could take to give time back to citizens (Strazdins & Innis, 2019). In our work together we came up with four steps, which the infographic illustrates.

1. First, build the evidence base about time use and time scarcity into policy thinking, from well-being indices (most contain time as a key marker of well-being) to routine data gathered on hours spent by citizens. This also means thinking about whose time might be affected.
2. Value time. By this we meant to change assumptions that time not paid is not valuable. We don't mean to place a dollar value on time (although this can be enlightening), so much as to view time spent caregiving, volunteering or looking after one's own health as well as others' as an important contribution, not to be wasted. For example, a 2018 survey found that most Australians would pay three times the minimum wage for an extra hour of time (NAB, 2018). For some people, time can be more valuable than money, and the government needs to treat it accordingly.
3. Define watch points or areas of regular policy development that might be adjusted to improve citizen time, such as work-family policies, or urban planning.
4. Finally, define the role governments, and other institutions, should take. Is it to free up time or to direct and nudge how people use their time (the latter is hardly likely to be welcomed, but the former most certainly would be).

The next section gives a few examples of where governments, urban planners, services and workplaces have used some of these principles and processes to create more time-sensitive interventions and policies (Fig. 4.1).

4.3 Some Examples

4.3.1 City Planning, Transport Systems and Neighbourhoods

Most urban policies or services are not designed to directly target health, but they can profoundly affect people's time. Reducing the time costs of everyday living could help to reduce the burdens on the time-poor, and while everybody might not use the 'saved' time for their health, many might, especially if the interventions intentionally embed health and time win-wins.

Smart city technology. Let's start with the idea of smart cities. Although almost all smart city initiatives foreground technology, the main goal is to save time. For example, 'One More Hour a Day' is the motto in Kalasatama, a smart city district of Helsinki, Finland, that aims to save one hour of resident's time every day (Helsinki Smart Region, 2018). By improving urban infrastructure with technology, smart cities can directly address the daily time costs of living to make cities more sustainable, healthy and efficient, ultimately improving quality of life for all residents (Steep & Nabi, 2016; Kamel Boulos & Al-Shorbaji, 2014). Kalasatama designers focused on saving time because, when they asked residents, it was what people said they wanted most. So, they developed new apps, made it quicker to park or access transport and relocated services to simplify and streamline so that the daily, necessary tasks of living, accessing health services and commuting were easier and faster.

Juniper, a research group on smart city innovations, has calculated the time-saving that a smart city approach could create. 125 hours, or 15 days, or three working weeks of time every year could be saved just by investing in technology (Juniper Research, 2018). Sixty hours could be

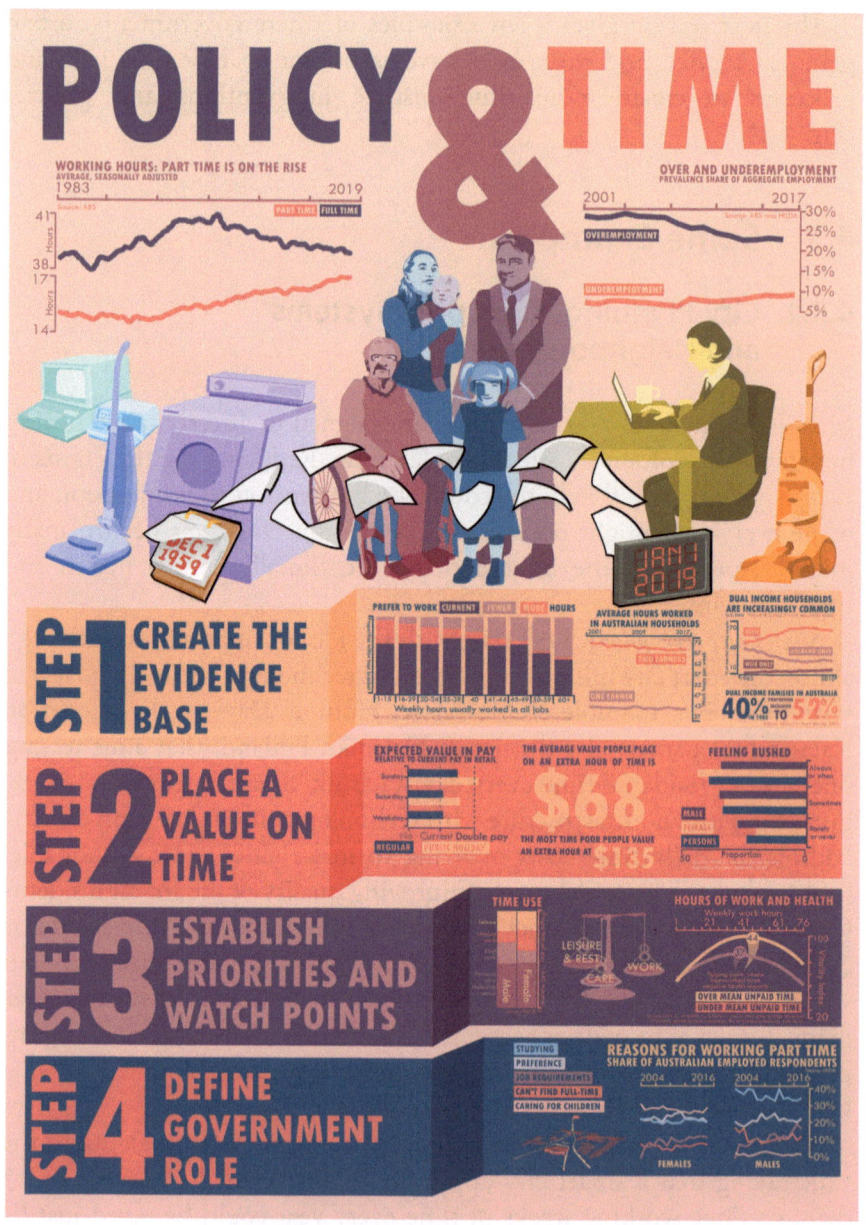

Fig. 4.1   How might governments give back time? Erin I Walsh 2019

saved by rolling out smart parking and better transport synchronisation; 35 hours could be saved from reduced disruptions due to crime or accidents and 9 hours could be saved from the use of mobile technology for health care. Smart city actions can also cut the time costs of health care by using open access scheduling, or investing in technology that enables telephone and email consultations (Intel, 2018). In emergency departments, investment in team-based models of care and better technology for registration, triage, identification and recording are shown to lower wait times (Ansell et al., 2017; Handel et al., 2011; Hoot & Aronsky, 2008; Shen & Lee, 2018).

Commutes and walkable neighbourhoods. Changing congested roads and long commutes could save time for drivers and it could help reduce social inequality. An Oxford team quantified travel times globally, finding that the longest trips to urban centres were found in the poorer countries (Weiss et al., 2018). But within countries, the inequality-time axiom also exists. Many people live in outer suburbs (where housing is cheaper) because they cannot afford to live in the centres close to workplaces, services and shops. North American and Australian cities are particularly marked by these socio-economic divisions between where people live and where they need to go to (work or school). The health consequences are profound. Not only does this increase car dependency (bad for air pollution), but it also locks in a sedentary lifestyle (time sitting in a car is not usable for health) and it is far more expensive (Tranter, 2010; Dodson & Sipe, 2007; Randolph & Holloway, 2005).

There's more. Better transport infrastructure could not only improve the health of those who drive, it could improve the health of those who walk. Pedestrian interaction with cars is a major disincentive for walking, which smart technology and better road design could change. In the New Zealand city of Auckland, for example, busy intersections were assessed in terms of the cost to pedestrians, and they were found to have added an extra 161 hours of delays to walking each year, a time cost that equates to a loss of NZ $200 million in productivity. No one explicitly calculated the health costs of that lost time walking, or the physical and mental weathering of feeling time stressed, but it was likely to be considerable (Lundberg et al., 2018).

Health is also a big winner when town planners design cities around walking instead of cars. There are so many benefits that flow from such an approach—and time is key to most of them. For example, a Liveable Neighbourhoods Community Design Code is a planning code which enables compact, walkable neighbourhoods and activity centres 5- and 10-minute walking distance from transport services and other facilities. The aim is to create neighbourhoods that encourage walking and foster sustainable and safe communities, embedding employment and services in residential areas. Streets are designed to make walking to work, school, shops or services as short, pleasant and safe as possible (Ker & Ginn, 2003). Equity can also be built into the design by ensuring there are seats to rest along the way for people with mobility difficulties, those pushing prams and the elderly. The win-win-win outcome for the environment, health and community connection are powerful. There is evidence that for every 10% increase in Liveable Neighbourhood compliance, people were 53% more likely to walk in their neighbourhoods, felt 40% safer from crime and their mental health improved by 14% (Bull et al., 2015).

Taking liveable neighbourhoods to the next level is embedding local sports clubs and venues in the areas that most need them (Estabrooks et al., 2003; Gordon-Larsen et al., 2006). To address the time, income and inequality barriers to sporting opportunities, the UK Doorstep Sports Clubs programme designed 'informal sports clubs that operate at the right time, for the right price, in the right place and in the right style'. The programme provided sporting opportunities to young people aged 14–25 years in extremely poor areas. The 100,000 plus participants in over 1000 different clubs across the UK in 2016/2017 gives a good indication of their success (StreetGames, 2018).

Active transport. Active transport programmes encourage less reliance on private cars and more on active alternatives like walking, cycling and public transport, offering another way to build physical activity into daily life. The goals of these programmes are explicitly about time, for example, "make physical activity achievable for people who don't have time" and also equity by reaching "population groups that are less likely to participate in leisure-time activity" (Wen et al., 2005; Heath et al., 2012). There are a few caveats, however. Not everyone uses their car for a single destination trip or have the physical mobility needed. Many parents combine their commute in the morning with dropping off children for childcare, then picking them up and doing shopping or other activities in the afternoon. And for some, using bicycles or buses is simply not an option.

Another widely used active transport programme targets children. A Walking School Bus is where groups of children regularly walk together to and from school along safe routes, under the supervision of an adult volunteer. For children, the benefits are multiple and well documented. Walking together to school helps build confidence about how to safely navigate local neighbourhoods, improves children's social and community connections and helps them keep physically active. With the right design, it can also alleviate time burdens on parents, but this rests on another caveat. Our review found that managing a Walking School Bus programme is time consuming (for schools or parents) and this meant they struggled to sustain them. Programmes that paid for time (e.g. paid parents, or allocated a paid staff member) seemed more stable. Another option is to seek local volunteers who have greater time resources (e.g. retirees) (Larouche et al., 2014; Victoria University, 2003; Mendoza et al., 2011; Heelan et al., 2009; Moodie et al., 2009).

4.3.2 Services

Less paperwork? Cass Sunstein in *Simpler* (2013) wrote about the future of government services. His vision was to simplify and streamline services so that the time (and money) cost to citizens, business and the state could go down. Fewer, smarter, simpler regulations and processes for citizens and business to interact with government sounds easy, but very few governments (or any bureaucratic institutions) seem to heed this. There are some exceptions, albeit with mixed evidence of success. In the US, the cumulative burden of paperwork is estimated at 11.6 billion hours. The US Paperwork Reduction Act aims to make the information collection more efficient and quicker (Administrative Conference of the United States, 2018). One way to do this was to estimate the time cost of each piece of paperwork or bureaucratic process, which is then given an economical value. Agencies are held accountable to these time costs and have performance goals to reduce them. Sounds good, although in practice it may not be that easy. One study found that the Act generates more paper-work by "creating bureaucracy that does paperwork on paperwork" (Samaha, 2015). Another evaluation found that the paperwork burdens were not much lower following the implementation of the Act, with com-pliance burdens estimated to cost small businesses $111 billion (however, economic cost estimates of citizen time were not undertaken) (House of Representatives United States, 2017). Proposed options include monetis-ing the costs of paperwork collection, meeting targeted reduction goals from Congress and moving more reporting requirements online. This evaluation was only from the perspective of small businesses though, and we could not find evaluations of the Act from citizen's perspectives.

Services in place. Healthy meals are time intensive because fresh food must be sourced, meals planned and then cooked and cleaned up, all of which presents a time challenge. Here are a couple of examples where childcare or workplaces can support some of the most time-stressed members of our community—employed mothers—through providing cheap and healthy food. Mothers in most nations are the primary food provisioners in households and those who are working or studying are among the most time-poor of all people. As one mother told us, "think-ing about something that everybody will eat, it's, that's the nightmare.... you get to the point where you can't think, I can't think what am I going to have tomorrow night for tea, let alone tonight, so I can't" (Mentha et al., 2020, p. 774). It's not only an issue for family nutrition, but also an issue for time equity.

Workplaces, schools and childcare centres offer a potential win-win that doesn't pit time to feed the family against earning income (or study-ing). In Denmark, for example, one initiative was to supply healthy and ready-to-heat takeaway meals in workplace canteens. They offer afford-able ways (considering both time and money) to support good nutrition for working families. These workplace canteen schemes not only take the time cost out of healthy eating but have additional health benefits such as lowering caloric intake, increasing vegetable intake, lowering blood pres-sure and prevalence of hypertension (Misawa et al., 2015; Thorsen et al., 2010; Vinholes et al., 2018; Lassen et al., 2012; Nordstrom, 2012; Mackison et al., 2016; Price et al., 2017). We also found examples of providing cheap, healthy meals at childcare and preschool which gave time as well as health gains. Children in these settings ate less fat and more fruit and vegetables which helped them maintain a healthy weight (Williams et al., 2002; Natale et al., 2017). The delivery of vaccination at schools and workplaces similarly saves time and leads to better immunisation rates. Even in homeplaces. For example, in Australia, routine childhood immunisations during home visits are particularly effective in remote Aboriginal and Torres Strait Islander communities (Ward et al., 2012). The evidence is consistent; offering vaccines at work or at school increases immunisation rates and they save time (Shahrabani & Benzion, 2010; Gidding et al., 2007). A health and time win-win.

Services after hours. Travel times, wait times, opening hours and competing responsibilities create a lose/lose situation for seeing doctors or other health care services for busy people (Ansell et al., 2017). There are quite a few studies showing that altering the timing of services to be more convenient, improves service access and reduces the time cost of using them. After-hours services are now widespread in many countries, and they can be combined with other, technology-supported options such as telehealth and digital services. One company in Australia provides telehealth and digital services as well as an after-hours GP helpline, which means consumers can consult doctors in the evenings, weekends and public holidays. They also offer a pregnancy, birth and baby service, which provides video-call access to maternal child health nurses so that parents do not need to leave their home or travel for face-to-face access to a health professional (Healthdirect Australia, 2018; Healthdirect Australia, 2017). These examples illustrate that reducing cost and distance barriers makes health care easier and feasible for those with any other restrictions on their time, which also makes health care fairer.

4.3.3 Workplaces

Bertrand Russell (1935, p. 29) in his essay in praise of idleness, observed that "modern methods of production have given us the possibility of ease and security for all; we have chosen, instead, to have overwork for some and starvation for others." It is fairly obvious that workplaces and industrial relations systems are fundamental to any strategy to free up time for health. It might also seem obvious that more health promotion in the workplace is the best way to do this. Ginny Sargent discovered when she studied health promotion in the workplace (in Chap. 2) that it isn't easy in practice. The very high value placed on employee time meant workplaces would rather give money for sports shoes or gym memberships than give an extra hour off. This pushed time for health promotion out of the workplace and into personal time. As Dr Sargent similarly found, employees were reluctant or unable to use time outside of their work hours to participate in extra health programmes. This see-sawing over whose time should be used reflects the political and economic basis of time on the job. It is not resolved, and pressures to increase time on the job haven't stopped.

This makes any attempt to change time in the workplace quite an exercise. Even now, despite the World Health Organization declaring long hours are one of the most impactful global health hazards, there are calls to make them even longer. In November 2023, for example, software billionaire NR Narayana Murthy (father-in-law of UK Prime Minister, Rishi Sunak) put forward the idea that young people in India should work 70 hours each week to help lift the country out of poverty.

But there are examples of countries and business leaders taking a different approach. Even a century ago, the approach taken by Henry Ford is illuminating. His motor vehicle factory had a turnover rate of 370%. This meant hiring 50,448 men in 1 year to maintain a workforce of around 14,000. Ford commissioned his personnel manager to investigate high turnover rates and absenteeism and he found the following drivers of this problem: long hours and exhaustion; low wages; poor housing conditions and family relationship breakdown; poor working conditions and bullying by supervisors. Ford's response? He instituted an 8-hour day, and a 40-hour week and a focus on worker health and well-being. Radical, not only in terms of payment, but in terms of hours and culture—his workers went from a 9- to 8-hour day at almost double the pay. The available evidence indicates quit rates fell by 87%, productivity increased by 30% and profits rose steadily (Raff & Summers, 1987). Ford claimed that doubling pay and cutting hours was one of the finest cost-cutting moves he had ever made.

There are also some national experiments in work hours, although with mixed results (and not much data on how health was affected). In 1982, with unemployment at 12%, the French government introduced a 39-hour full-time working week with an additional fifth paid week vacation (De Spiegelaere & Piasna, 2017). In 1988 they then reduced this further, to 35 hours. There were no cuts to wages (Hayden, 2006) and it is estimated that up to half a million jobs were created. There were social equity benefits, (more older workers entered the labour market and more women increased their hours), but workloads didn't always go down, so the pace of work went up. It didn't last, and as the national government changed hands, the 35-hour week returned to 40 hours. The Netherlands also enacted legislation to combat long work hours and created the world's first 'part-time economy' with approximately 47% of all employees working part time. However, as in most countries, it was women and not men who opted for the part-time jobs, while men continued to populate the long hour, higher paying jobs.

Less time on? Six-hour days or 4-day working weeks are two options on the table. There are lots of hesitancies and these are understandable. Despite claims to the contrary, interventions like a 4-day working week have the potential to cost more, and this could make some businesses unviable if their competitors don't follow suit. There is also no guarantee they will improve gender equity if the long hours (and highly paid) jobs that are most worked by men are not reined in at the same time. But there are examples where countries and workplaces trialled reduced hours or days of working to improve work-life balance, gender equality and create more time for people to be healthy. The evidence seems quite consistent—health generally improves.

Six-hour working days have been piloted in Sweden (Booker, 2015; Winroth, 2017; Erlandsson & Sundberg, 2016) and Finland (Anttila et al., 2005; Peltola, 1998) and both evaluations find that the reduction in hours had numerous health benefits with decreased stress levels, improved sleep, increased physical activity and increased satisfaction, in addition to less sick days taken and stable or boosted productivity. Employees in Sweden did not have any reductions in pay but employees in Finland took pay cuts. In the Swedish project, new staff were needed to cover the 'lost' hours and this cost was, at the time, covered by the government. This undermined the sustainability of this reduced hours experiment and as such, it was no longer continued.

A reduction in days worked per week has also been found to have health benefits. For example, a New Zealand company, Perpetual Guardian, trialled a 4-day (paid 5-day) working week with employees reporting better work-life balance, and lower stress levels (Haar, 2018; Barnes PGC, 2019).

There is also a vast amount of research evidence on the benefits to employee health of more flexible working (flexible hours, working from home, part-time options) which I covered in Chap. 2. The evidence on health benefits of more recent interventions such as the right to disconnect and hybrid working is less mature, but these interventions, theoretically at least, should help with time stresses from long commutes and combining work and caregiving.

I end with an example of workplaces 'giving time' to care, which I know well, as I had the good fortune to be part of the evaluation team led by the late Bill Martin (Martin et al., 2011).

(Paid) time to care. In 2011, Australia achieved its first legislated paid parental leave scheme. It was the second last OECD nation to do so. This late start was a function of our history, politics and eventually the need to support more women to work and enable a more productive economy. At that time, the country had low fertility and there were concerns about how to support a rapidly ageing and expanding population. Before then, we had a complex system of leave with legislated unpaid leave of up to 2 years, but some mothers, who held highly skilled or valued jobs, also had workplace-specific paid leave. The legislated, whole of population intervention in 2011 explicitly coupled money supports to mothers (payment) with time supports (18 weeks leave away from work). Almost all low-skilled and low-paid mothers in casual or insecure employment received no paid-leave entitlements at all. At best, these mothers could apply for unpaid parental leave which gave them time but required a trade-off of money (lost earnings).

We found that this coupling of time with money in the policy design improved Australian mothers' health across a range of dimensions, including mental and physical health (Hewitt et al., 2017). It also had a social equity impact. Casually employed mothers (those without any secure job contracts) showed better mental health scores than their counterparts whose health we assessed the year before the scheme started. Perhaps not surprisingly, the mothers who fared the very best were the most economically advantaged. They added their workplace paid leave onto the government funded 18 weeks, giving them much longer to recover from the birth, bond with their baby and breastfeed without losing income. They were also less time stressed.

This paid time intervention made for a win-win, and it likely had a generational impact (Fig. 4.2). Although the babies were too young for us to really assess their health, we did find that the longer mothers had paid time-off, breastfeeding rates improved. There are other studies (in other countries and contexts) showing how both parent and child health improves when parents have access to paid leave (Tanaka, 2005; Berger et al., 2005). The Australian scheme is of course far less generous than many others, and it has been recently extended. There are other approaches being taken by countries to create win-wins for fathers as well. Iceland is a stellar example.

Fig. 4.2 Girl with clock (after De Chirico). 2024 Author

4.4 Conclusion

Do we have a right to time for our health? Fitzpatrick (2004) argued that "the right to meaningful time is a basic human right... for without adequate temporal space to act, interact, speak and think, all of the other rights are correspondingly weakened" (p. 148). The desire to do and produce more-faster-cheaper has been a motivation that has empowered nations and corporations, we have all become richer by asking more of people and of the planet. So, it is a curious moment of history—post-pandemic—in which to be ending this chapter and book.

Because the COVID-19 pandemic led to a virtual shutdown of almost all countries and economies, in the matter of a few weeks, people, businesses and nations were told to stop. Do not do more. Stay home, shut down, don't travel and for some—don't work; whatever the cost to protect health (although the 'invisible work' of caregiving did not receive the same permission to stop, indeed many parents added home schooling to their load). Almost everything that we normally did with our time was questioned; can it wait, be paused, hibernate or simply end until we know health is safe?

This was, for a short period, an extraordinary, upside-down acknowledgement of how important health was. The pandemic showed that health is not something that can be taken for granted and it meant, briefly, that the economic drivers of decisions were suborned to protect health. Everyone needed to figure out a new balance between lives and livelihoods. It hasn't stuck though.

So, could we possibly free up more time? It might be costly in terms of productivity, at least in the short term. It would be hard, certainly, to change a mindset and set of practices about valuing time outside of the market as well as time within it. Even if there are short-term economic costs, the long-term benefits of good health and greater equality could mean a stronger economy and a happier, fairer society, maybe. If we thought more about time and valued it by how cities are built, what work hours are expected, how important time for care is and especially how everyone needs time for enough rest, exercise, healthy food and connection to others, we could reduce the slow, quiet and deadly pandemics that are still unravelling—cancer, cardiovascular illness, diabetes type 2, metabolic disorders, depression, anxiety and diseases of despair. I hope this chapter has given some principles and possibilities that could support the right to enough time for health.

References

Administrative Conference of the United States. Paperwork Reduction Act Efficiencies, 83 Fed Reg 30,683, 30,683. (2018). https://www.acus.gov/research-projects/paperwork-reduction-act-efficiencies

Ansell, D., Crispo, J. A. G., Simard, B., & Bjerre, L. M. (2017). Interventions to reduce wait times for primary care appointments: A systematic review. *BMC Health Services Research, 17*(1), 295.

Anttila, T., Nätti, J., & Väisänen, M. (2005). The experiments of reduced working hours in Finland: Impact on work–family interaction and the importance of the sociocultural setting. *Community, Work & Family, 8*(2), 187–209.

Barnes PGC, Auckland University of Technology UoA, Watts MER. (2019). *White Paper: The four-day week: Guidelines for an outcome-based trial: Raising productivity and engagement.*

Beagle, P. S. (2022). *The last unicorn* (3rd ed.). ACE Publishers.

Berger, L. M., Hill, J., & Waldfogel, J. (2005). Maternity leave, early maternal employment and child health and development in the US. *The Economic Journal, 115*(501), F29–F47.

Booker, C. (2015). Sweden is moving towards a six hour working day as Australia's hours increase. *Sydney Morning Herald.* https://www.smh.com.au/business/workplace/sweden-is-moving-toards-a-six-hour-working-day-as-australias-hours-increase-20151001-gjyp33.html

Bull, F., Hooper, P., Foster, S., Giles-Corti, B., & the RESIDE team. (2015). *Living liveable. The impact of the liveable neighbourhoods policy on the health and wellbeing of Perth residents.* The University of Western Australia.

Burkeman, O. (2021). *Four thousand weeks: Time management for mortals.* Farrow, Status and Giroux.

Davis, G. C., & You, W. (2011). Not enough money or not enough time to satisfy the Thrifty Food Plan? A cost difference approach for estimating a money–time threshold. *Food Policy, 36*(2), 101–107.

De Spiegelaere, S., & Piasna, A. (2017). *The why and how of working time reduction.* European Trade Union Institute.

Dodson, J., & Sipe, N. (2007). Oil vulnerability in the Australian city: Assessing socioeconomic risks from higher urban fuel prices. *Urban Studies, 44*(1), 37–62.

Dumka, L. E., Garza, C. A., Roosa, M. W., & Stoerzinger, H. D. (1997). Recruitment and retention of high-risk families into a preventive parent training intervention. *Journal of Primary Prevention, 18*(1), 25–39.

Erlandsson, M., & Sundberg, M. (2016). *From eight hours working day to six hours working day with retained salary. An explorative study of mental well-being, stress, occupational involvement and time spent on healthcare professionals.* Lund University.

Estabrooks, P. A., Lee, R. E., & Gyurcsik, N. C. (2003). Resources for physical activity participation: Does availability and accessibility differ by neighbourhood socioeconomic status? *Annals of Behavioral Medicine, 25*(2), 100–104.

Fitzpatrick, T. (2004). Social policy and time. *Time & Society, 13*(2-3), 197–219. https://doi.org/10.1177/0961463X04043502

Gidding, H. F., Warlow, M., MacIntyre, C. R., Backhouse, J., Gilbert, G. L., Quinn, H. E., et al. (2007). The impact of a new universal infant and school-based adolescent hepatitis B vaccination program in Australia. *Vaccine, 25*(51), 8637–8641.

Gordon-Larsen, P., Nelson, M. C., Page, P., & Popkin, B. M. (2006). Inequality in the built environment underlies key health disparities in physical activity and obesity. *Pediatrics, 117*(2), 417–424.

Haar, J. (2018). *Overview of the perpetual guardian 4-day (paid 5) work trial [Industry report]*. Auckland University of Technology.

Handel, D., Epstein, S., Khare, R. K., Abernethy, D., Klauer, K., Pilgrim, R., et al. (2011). Interventions to improve the timeliness of emergency care. *American Emergency Medicine, 18*(12), 1295–1302.

Hayden, A. (2006). France's 35-hour week: Attack on business? Win-win reform? Or betrayal of disadvantaged workers? *Politics and Society, 34*(4), 503–542.

Healthdirect Australia. (2017). *Annual report. Business highlights 2016–2017.*

Healthdirect Australia. *Equity of access for all Australians Sydney 2018.* Accessed August 20, 2018., from https://about.healthdirect.gov.au/equity-of-access-for-all-australians

Heath, G. W., Parra, D. C., Sarmiento, O. L., Andersen, L. B., Owen, N., Goenka, S., et al. (2012). Evidence-based intervention in physical activity: Lessons from around the world. *Lancet, 380*(9838), 272–281.

Heelan, K. A., Abbey, B. M., Donnelly, J. E., Mayo, M. S., & Welk, G. J. (2009). Evaluation of a walking school bus for promoting physical activity in youth. *Journal of Physical Activity and Health, 6*(5), 560–567.

Helsinki Smart Region. (2018). Health & Wellness Helsinki: Helsinki-Uusimaa Regional Council. Accessed August 15, 2018, from https://www.helsinkismart.fi/human-health-tech/

Hewitt, B., Strazdins, L., & Martin, W. (2017). The benefits of paid maternity leave for mothers' post-partum health and wellbeing: Evidence from an Australian evaluation. *Social Science and Medicine, 182,* 97–105. https://doi.org/10.1016/j.socscimed.2017.04.022

Hoot, N. R., & Aronsky, D. (2008). Systematic review of emergency department crowding: Causes, effects, and solutions. *Annals of Emergency Medicine, 52*(2), 126–36.e1.

Intel. (2018). *Infographic: Time savings with smart cities.* Enterprise Innovation. Accessed September 11, 2018, from https://www.enterpriseinnovation.net/infographic/infographic-time-savings-smart-cities

Juniper Research. *Smart cities technologies give back 125 hours to citizens every year 2018.* Accessed October 4, 2018., from https://newsroom.intel.com/news/smart-cities-iot-research-125-hours/

Kamel Boulos, M. N., & Al-Shorbaji, N. M. (2014). On the internet of things, smart cities and the WHO healthy cities. *International Journal of Health Geographics, 13,* 10.

Ker, L., & Ginn, S. (2003). Myths and realities in walkable catchments: The case of walking and transit. *Road and Transport Research Journal, 12*(2), 69–80.

Larouche, R., Saunders, T. J., Faulkner, G., Colley, R., & Tremblay, M. (2014). Associations between active school transport and physical activity, body composition, and cardiovascular fitness: A systematic review of 68 studies. *Journal of Physical Activity and Health, 11*(1), 206–227.

Lassen, A. D., Ernst, L., Poulsen, S., Andersen, K. K., Hansen, G. L., Biltoft-Jensen, A., et al. (2012). Effectiveness of a canteen take away concept in promoting healthy eating patterns among employees. *Public Health Nutrition, 15*(3), 452–458.

Lundberg, K., Nunns, P., Houghton, S., Rohani, M., Cagney, M. R., & Auckland Council. (2018). *Business case for walking: Counting walking to make walking count in Auckland.* Engineering NZ.

Mackison, D., Mooney, J., Macleod, M., & Anderson, A. S. (2016). Lessons learnt from a feasibility study on price incentivised healthy eating promotions in workplace catering establishments. *Journal of Human Nutrition and Dietetics, 29*(1), 86–94.

Martin, B., Hewitt, B., Baird, M., Baxter, J., Heron, A., Whitehouse, G., Zadoroznyj, M., Xiang, N., Broom, D., Connelly, L., Jones, A., Kalb, G., McVicar, D., Strazdins, L., Walter, M., Western, M., & Wooden, M. (2011). *Paid parental leave phase 1 baseline report.* Occasional paper no. 44, Department of Families, Housing, Community Services and Indigenous Affairs.

Mendoza, J. A., Watson, K., Baranowski, T., Nicklas, T. A., Uscanga, D. K., & Hanfling, M. J. (2011). The walking school bus and children's physical activity: A pilot cluster randomized controlled trial. *Pediatrics, 128*(3), e537–e544. https://doi.org/10.1542/peds.2010-3486

Mentha, K., Booth, S., Coveny, J., & Strazdins, L. (2020). Feeding the Australian family: Challenges for mothers, nutrition, and equity. *Health Promotion International, 35*(4), 771–778.

Misawa, A., Yoshita, K., Fukumura, T., Tanaka, T., Tamaki, J., Takebayashi, T., et al. (2015). Effects of a long-term intervention in a work cafeteria on employee vegetable intake. *Sangyō eiseigaku zasshi, Journal of Occupational Health, 57*(3), 97–107.

Moodie, M., Haby, M., Galvin, L., Swinburn, B., & Carter, R. (2009). Cost-effectiveness of active transport for primary school children – Walking school bus program. *International Journal of Behavioral Nutrition and Physical Activity, 6*(1), 63.

Natale, R. A., Messiah, S. E., Asfour, L. S., Uhlhorn, S. B., Englebert, N. E., & Arheart, K. L. (2017). Obesity prevention program in childcare centers: Two-year follow-up. *American Journal of Health Promotion, 31*(6), 502–510.

National Australia Bank Behavioural & Industry Economics. (2018). *NAB well-being insight report. Time: How we use it & value it.* National Australia Bank.

Nordström, J. (2012). Willingness to pay for wholesome canteen takeaway. *Appetite, 58*(1), 168–179.

Pega, F., Náfrádi, B., Momen, N. C., Ujita, Y., Streicher, K. N., Prüss-Üstün, A., Descatha, A., Driscoll, T., Fischer, F. M., Godderis, L., Kiiver, H. M., Li, J., Magnusson Hanson, L. L., Ruglies, R., Sørensen, K., & Woodruff, T. J. (2021). Global, regional, and national burdens of ischemic heart disease and stroke attributable to exposure to long working hours for 194 countries, 2000–2016: A systematic analysis from the WHO/ILO Joint Estimates of the Work-related Burden of Disease and Injury. *Environment International, 154.* https://doi.org/10.1016/j.envint.2021.106595

Peltola, P. (1998). Working time reduction in Finland. *Transfer: European Review of Labour and Research, 4*(4), 729–746.

Price, S., Bray, J., & Brown, L. (2017). Enabling healthy food choices in the workplace: The canteen operators' perspective. *International Journal of Workplace Health Management, 10*(4), 318–331.

Raff, D. M., & Summers, L. H. (1987). Did Henry Ford pay efficiency wages? *Journal of Labor Economics, 5*(4, Part 2), S57–S86.

Randolph, B., & Holloway, D. (2005). Social disadvantage, tenure and location: An analysis of Sydney and Melbourne. *Urban Policy and Research, 23*(2), 173–201.

Russell, B. (1935). *In praise of idleness (and other essays).* Allen and Unwin.

Samaha, A. M. (2015). Death and paperwork reduction. *Duke Law Journal, 65*(2), 279–344.

Shahrabani, S., & Benzion, U. (2010). Workplace vaccination and other factors impacting influenza vaccination decision among employees in Israel. *International Journal of Environmental Research and Public Health, 7*(3), 853–869.

Shen, Y., & Lee, L. H. (2018). Improving the wait time to consultation at the emergency department. *BMJ Open Quality, 7*(1), e000131.

Steep, M., & Nabi, M. (2016). Smart cities improve the health of their citizens. *Forbes.* Accessed August 15, 2018, from https://www.forbes.com/sites/mikesteep/2016/06/27/can-smart-cities-improve-the-health-of-its-citizens/#40108c5d3957

Strazdins, L, & Ford, L. (2019) *Cities for our time: Policies, programs and services to address time constraints on health and wellbeing.*

Strazdins, L., & Innis, S. (2019, July 4). Most people don't have enough time in their lives. Here's how government can help them get some of it back. Published as a Mandarin Premium expert briefing. *The Mandarin.* https://www.themandarin.com.au/111032-most-people-dont-have-enough-time-in-their-lives-heres-how-government-can-help-them-get-some-of-it-back/

Strazdins, L., Lucas, N., Shipley, M., Mathews, B., Berry, H. L., Rodgers, B., & Davies, A. (2012). Parent and child wellbeing and the influence of work and family arrangements: A three cohort study. *FaHCSIA Social Policy Research Paper,* (44).

StreetGames. (2018). *Doorstep sports clubs Manchester.* StreetGames UK. Accessed November 1, 2018, from https://network.streetgames.org/our-work/doorstep-sport-clubs

Sunstein, C. R. (2013). *Simpler: The future of government.* Simon and Schuster.

Tanaka, S. (2005). Parental leave and child health across OECD countries. *The Economic Journal, 115*(501), F7–F28.

Thorsen, A. V., Lassen, A. D., Tetens, I., Hels, O., & Mikkelsen, B. E. (2010). Long-term sustainability of a worksite canteen intervention of serving more fruit and vegetables. *Public Health Nutrition, 13*(10), 1647–1652.

Tranter, P. J. (2010). Speed kills: The complex links between transport, lack of time and urban health. *Journal of Urban Health: Bulletin of the New York Academy of Medicine, 87*(2), 155–166.

Victoria University. (2003). *The walking school bus program: Learnings from Vichealth's pilot program 2001*. Victorian Health Promotion Foundation.

United States House of Representatives. (2017). *Evaluating the Paperwork Reduction Act: Are burdens being reduced?: Hearing before the Committee on Small Business, United States House of Representatives, First session*.

Vinholes, D. B., Machado, C. A., Chaves, H., Rossato, S. L., Melo, I., Fuchs, F. D., et al. (2018). Workplace staff canteen is associated with lower blood pressure among industry workers. *British Food Journal, 120*(3), 602–612.

Ward, K., Chow, M. Y. K., King, C., & Leask, J. (2012). Strategies to improve vaccination uptake in Australia, a systematic review of types and effectiveness. *Australian and New Zealand Journal of Public Health, 36*(4), 369–377.

Weiss, D., Nelson, A., Gibson, H., et al. (2018). A global map of travel time to cities to assess inequalities in accessibility in 2015. *Nature, 553*, 333–336. https://doi.org/10.1038/nature25181

Wen, L. M., Orr, N., Bindon, J., & Rissel, C. (2005). Promoting active transport in a workplace setting: Evaluation of a pilot study in Australia. *Health Promotion International, 20*(2), 123–133.

Williams, C. L., Bollella, M. C., Strobino, B. A., Spark, A., Nicklas, T. A., Tolosi, L. B., et al. (2002). "Healthy-start": Outcome of an intervention to promote a heart healthy diet in preschool children. *Journal of the American College of Nutrition, 21*(1), 62–71.

Winroth, C. (2017). *6-hour working day: The Swedish story*. EuroCite. Note n°16. http://eurocite.eu/wp-content/uploads/2017/04/Winroth-6-hour-working-day-Sweden.pdf

References

(2017). *Evaluating the Paperwork Reduction Act: Are burdens being reduced?: Hearing before the Committee on Small Business, United States House of Representatives, First session.*

Christian, H., Knuiman, M., Bull, F., Timperio, A., Foster, S., Divitini, M., et al. (2013). A new urban planning code's impact on walking: The residential environments project. *American Journal of Public Health, 103*(7), 1219–1228.

Davies, K. (2001). Responsibility and daily life. In J. May & N. Thrift (Eds.), *Timespace: Geographies of temporality* (pp. 133–148). Routledge.

Harvard International Office. (2020). *Getting to know Americans.* https://www.hio.harvard.edu/getting-know-americans

Reid, K. (2019). *Walk for water: You 6K vs. theirs.* https://www.worldvision.org/clean-water-news-stories/walk-water-6k

Strazdins, L., Doan, T., Leach, L., Li, J., Pollmann-Schult, M., & Kaiser, T. (n.d.). *Ceilings: Hours, health and gender inequality in earnings.* Under review.

StreetGames. (2017). *Annual report.* StreetGames UK. https://network.streetgames.org/sites/default/files/SG%20Annual%20Report%20for%20year%20ended%2031%20March%202017.pdf

Sugiyama, T., Francis, J., Middleton, N., Owen, N., & Giles-Corti, B. (2010). Associations between recreational walking and attractiveness, size, and proximity of neighbourhood open spaces. *American Journal of Public Health, 100*(9), 1752–1757.

Trumbo, P., Schlicker, S., Yates, A. A., & Poos, M. (2002). Dietary reference intakes for energy, carbohydrate, fiber, fat, fatty acids, cholesterol, protein and amino acids. *Journal of the American Dietetic Association, 102*(11), 1621–1630. https://doi.org/10.1016/S0002-8223(02)90346-9

Wardman, M. (2004). Public transport values of time. *Transport Policy, 11*(4), 363–377.

Index[1]

---

[1] Note: Page numbers followed by 'n' refer to notes.

© The Author(s), under exclusive license to Springer Nature Singapore Pte Ltd. 2024   **109**
L. Strazdins, *The Unequal Hour*, https://doi.org/10.1007/978-981-97-6337-5